JOURNEY OF FAITH

in

SANTA MARIA, CALIFORNIA.

A HISTORY OF SOME CHURCHES.

By

OLLIE M. KIRBY

JANAWAY PUBLISHING, INC.
Santa Maria, California
2011

Published by
Janaway Publishing, Inc.
732 Kelsey Ct.
Santa Maria, California 93454
(805) 925-1038
www.JanawayPublishing.com

2011

ISBN: 978-1-59641-249-1

Cover photograph of painting by John Gardner Doty courtesy of Dottie Lyons.

Made in the United States of America

CONTENTS

PREFACE

The purpose for writing this book is straightforward: ALL of us are children of God, and anything that divides us is not nearly as powerful as that which unites us. *Journey of Faith in Santa Maria, California*, highlights the wonderful influence ALL of the churches, individually and collectively, have had (and continue to have) in the formation, development and growth of the Santa Maria Valley.

This book is organized by church, with the history and information on each church contained in a single chapter, and, to the extent possible, placed in the order in which they were founded. For example, there were five of the churches which were established in the 1800s, so they comprise the first five chapters.

All of the information, and most of the photographs, in this book were provided by each individual church. For example, some of the churches provided information, notes, and documents which were the source for the narrative of their history. Alternatively, several churches submitted final copy, or near final copy, which was used as the finished text for a specific chapter.

I hope you enjoy reading this book as much as I enjoyed writing it. Let the journey begin!

Ollie M. Kirby
Santa Maria, California
November 1, 2011

ACKNOWLEDGEMENTS

A special thanks to the following individuals:

1. Margaret Doty, whose loving faith in me, and assistance, made this book possible.

2. My husband, Eldon Kirby, whose proof-reading and patience were invaluable throughout this past year.

3. Dottie Lyons, whose wonderful photography and assistance were indispensable in the cover design.

4. Gene Corbin, whose computer expertise was essential. He had to have infinite patience with me, especially in the very beginning.

5. Jim Skidmore of Janaway Publishing, Inc. He was a godsend and guided me through the maze of the entire process. Thank God for a local publisher!

And last, but certainly not least, thanks to all the people of the churches involved for their overwhelming cooperation and input in the production of this book. It was a labor of love. Words can't describe the experience. For nearly a year I "ate, slept, and breathed" the writing of this book.

This book is dedicated to

ALL THE PEOPLE OF FAITH

in

SANTA MARIA, CALIFORNIA

CHAPTER ONE

FIRST UNITED METHODIST CHURCH

In a world filled with an explosion of change, there is a place where the old and new meld together as seamlessly as a beautiful old tapestry.

That place is First United Methodist Church in the West Town Center Mall in Santa Maria, California.

The Methodist society was first organized May 7, 1873, in a scattered settlement frequently referred to as Grangerville. When a town site was laid out in 1874, however, the "founding fathers" designated it as "Central City." It wasn't until 1882 that the town was renamed "Santa Maria." There was no church building, so the society worshipped in Fleisher's Hall part of the time and in the Pleasant Valley schoolhouse the rest of the time.

In 1878, the Methodist Episcopal finally were able to build a church house at the northeast corner of what is now Lincoln and Church Streets. It was a rough wooden frame structure 24' by 40'. The lumber was hauled by wagon from Point Sal. Soon afterward, the belfry was built on the front of the church to house the bell that was salvaged from the ANNA LYLE, a $20,000 schooner on its maiden voyage from San Francisco, which was destroyed along with the Point Sal wharf in a severe storm on Christmas night of 1876. That bell was moved to each subsequent new building and still hangs in their bell tower today.

Fourteen years later (1892), a grand new building with stained glass windows was erected across the street on the northwest corner of Lincoln and Church Streets. This building was sold to J.U. Northman in 1921, with the proviso that the Methodists could occupy it until their new building was completed in 1922. Since the building went into private ownership, the church archives do not have a record of when it was razed, but there is a record of the fact that one church member salvaged some of the pieces of stained glass. From those pieces of stained glass, he fashioned a beautiful triangular-shaped light which is in their church today.

The magnificent Spanish Renaissance style structure you see today at the corner of Cook and Broadway was built in 1922. Old photographs (circa 1929) show the gas station that was located on the corner of the church lot. The income from that gas station helped keep the church afloat during some very difficult times. At the expiration of the oil company's lease in December 1963, the service station was razed, tanks removed, and the lot was cleared and landscaped. A picture from the Santa Maria Times shows the heavy flooding that occurred in 1941 on that corner in front of the service station.

At the time of construction, the basements were left unfinished. The floors were just dirt, and the Men's Brotherhood played horseshoes in the north side. During the thirties, a large amount of dirt was taken out of the south basement by a crew of volunteer men. The floor was cemented over and used as a skating rink, and for general recreation (including servicemen) during World War II. Soon after the war, it was closed because of fire danger and not reopened until construction, a few years later, of an additional entrance and fire doors.

There was a lighted (and originally revolving) cross operating atop the church. This was a memorial to the servicemen of the community. Funding for this was raised in 1921. The cross served as a beacon for the pilots who were training at Camp Cook. That cross had to be replaced with a new cross at the time of the church remodeling. The cross which is now atop the building neither lights nor rotates.

The sanctuary contains NINE harmonizing stained glass memorial windows inscribed with the names of the following founders/members: John Newlove; Maria B. Newlove; George and Lydia Stowell; J. R. and Mary T. Norris; T. C. Nance; C. C. Oakley; Laura Wylie Ruoff; Nora B. Hawthorne; and Corp. Marshall N. Braden.

The 1986 Earthquake Hazards Reduction Act brought about a major crisis for the church: either overhaul/reinforce the existing structure, or tear it down.

The church opted to upgrade and expand at its present location. An approximately $1.3 million restoration and expansion project was completed in May 1996. Although the sanctuary was enlarged and the altar area remodeled, the design continuity is flawless. And EVERYONE agrees that the new pews are more comfortable than the old folding seats, which were from a theater which was torn down!

The new entrance off the Town Center West parking lot and the narthex demonstrate the "new face" of the church. The NEW stained glass memorial windows in the narthex are alive with vibrant colors and design.

In 1997, a mighty, new 2,379-pipe organ was completed. This is the second largest pipe organ on the Central Coast.

In 2010, a completely new sound system was installed as a memorial to the late John Gardner Doty. There is now a great sound system to do justice to all the church's great music.

The Methodist church has been here in the heart of Santa Maria continuously throughout its history. First it was in a community known as Grangerville; then it was in Central City; and now Santa Maria. It has played a vital role in the social and economic development of Santa Maria. And it has remained downtown.

FIRST METHODIST EPISCOPAL CHURCH

FIRST CHURCH ERECTED IN 1878
Lumber used in building was slavaged from ship wrecked off Point Sal.

CHURCH BELL SALVAGED FROM THE *ANNA LYLE*
*The church bell was salvaged from the scooner, "Anna Lyle," soon after completion of construction
of the church in 1878. This bell was moved to each subsequent new building and still hangs in the bell tower today.*

SECOND CHURCH ERECTED IN 1892.
This was the First United Methodist Church's second building, completed in 1892. Photograph circa 1905

PRESENT FIRST UNITED METHODIST CHURCH BUILDING.
The third and present facility was built in 1922 at the corner of Cook and Broadway. Photograph circa 1929

SANTA MARIA, CALIFORNIA,   THURSDAY, FEBRUARY 13, 41   18 PAGES THIS WEEK

Everyone Catches His Limit When the Steelhead Run up Cook Creek

---Photo by Karleski

Remember When ???

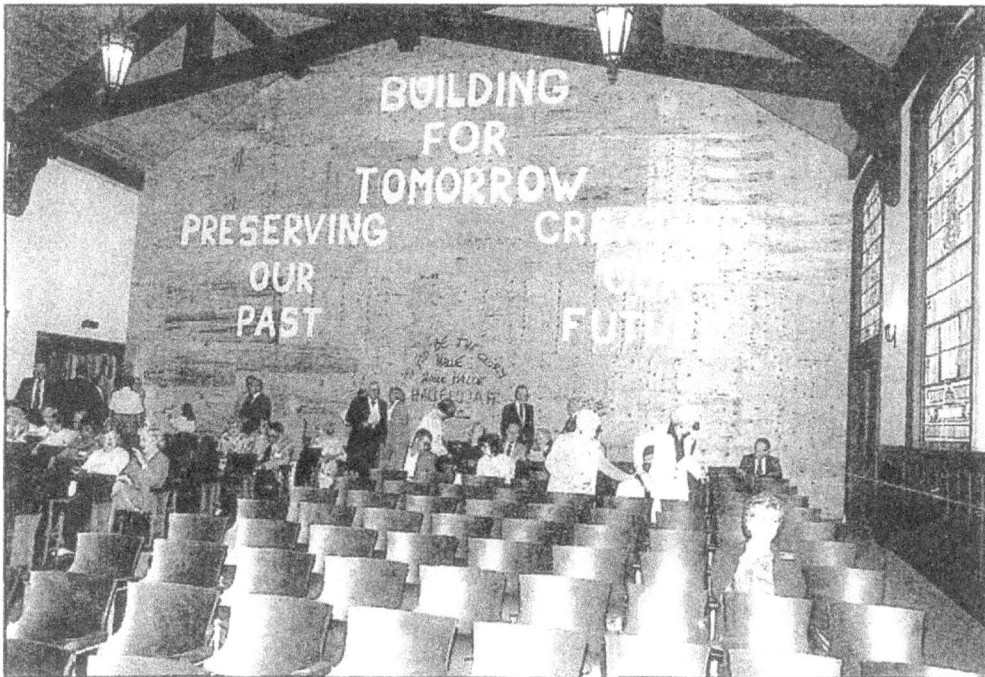

BUILDING
FOR
TOMORROW
PRESERVING
OUR
PAST

Photograph circa 1995

FILIPINO CHOIR, FIRST UNITED METHODIST CHURCH, 2011

CHAPTER TWO

SANTA MARIA PRESBYTERIAN CHURCH

EARLY HISTORY

The chartering of the First Presbyterian Church occurred August 7, 1876, as the First Presbyterian Church of Guadalupe by the Rev. Thomas Fraser, Missionary Agent of the Synod of the Pacific. The church had to meet in Guadalupe until they could obtain a place to hold their services in Santa Maria.

On January 30, 1882, three lots were purchased on the corner of Chapel and Vine for the purpose of erecting a church and parsonage. There is an old photo taken by Tommy Rice of the first church building erected on that property.

The Ladies Aid Society of the church purchased a lot, 75' X 173', at the corner of Cook and Lincoln on March 15, 1911, for $1,050. The church building erected on this corner was dedicated on March 13, 1913. When a new church building was erected in 1911, the lots on Chapel and Vine Streets were sold.

A picture of this second church building was found in a cookbook published in 1922, put together by the Ladies Aid Society of the Presbyterian Church. That old cookbook is still in existence today and is owned by Jane (Adam) Drenon. She allowed the copying of the old photo, as well as the cover of the cookbook. The cookbook was a gift from her aunt, Mrs. Arthur E. (Viola) Jessee. Cookbooks sold for $2.00 in 1922. Ten years later (1932) cookbooks still sold for $2.00!

The old photo in the cookbook showed the original construction. The original design had to be modified somewhat at the top, as special ornamentation at the top in several locations leaked badly and could not be corrected. A photo (included) shows the design change, especially at the top of the tower, to correct the problem.

In September 1958, a lot was purchased at the corner of Cook and Pine Streets. The cost was $13,500. Property for the Christian Education Building was purchased in April 1952. Dedication of the Christian Education Building took place on March 13, 1955. Cost was $80,979.00. This was the first building on the new site, and it is still in use today; the Church Office is located in this building.

The lot west of the Christian Education Building was purchased for $11,500 in November 1957. The cornerstone was laid November 24, 1957, for Westminster Hall. Dedication occurred April 13, 1958.

The current sanctuary on Cook Street was built in 1961 at a cost of $195,000, and was dedicated February 17, 1962.

The   John Calvin Chapel was dedicated February 19, 1967, honoring the magnificent art work by Dr. John Karamitsos in memory of their daughter.

Completion of the beautiful stained glass windows in the sanctuary was in 1968 and dedicated on July 21, 1968.

The mortgage on the sanctuary was paid in full on May 10, 1971.

A Hispanic ministry was established in 1983 with Rev. Tom Martinez, who was followed by Osvaldo Fiallo.

Church records indicate the purchase of property at 406 South Pine Street at a cost of $25,000.   There was a small house on the lot.   This structure was fixed up and later rented for a short time for use as a homeless shelter.

BEGINNINGS OF THE HOMELESS SHELTER IN SANTA MARIA

The Homeless Shelter actually had its beginnings January 31, 1986, according to Mickey Keith who has worked in it since its inception.   It started with the Presbyterians letting the homeless bed down on mats in their Fellowship Hall overnight.   Some member of the congregation (often the minister!) would have to remain there overnight and monitor the operation.   It started out with just a few guests but soon grew to be too many.   Something had to be done.

Four single-wide mobile homes were purchased, and put together (with modifications) and placed in the parking lot of the Presbyterian Church.   Mickey recalls that several other churches were involved - Bethel Lutheran, Orcutt Presbyterian, and First Christian.

Today, the entire operation is run by the Good Samaritan Shelter on West Morrison. Various churches, non-profit and civic organizations, and even Marian Hospital take turns feeding the homeless and working at the shelter.   One separate building is the Detox Center and is more closely monitored.

Mickey Keith of the Presbyterian church has devoted much of her life since 1986 to working with the homeless.   GOD BLESS HER!

MORE RECENT CHURCH HISTORY

In September 1992 a contemporary Praise and Worship Service was added to the Sunday morning schedule.   And today there is one combined service, not two separate services.

On February 27, 2011, Pastor Israel Gonzales participated in a "Pulpit Exchange", when six clergy traded churches for a Sunday morning.   It gave all the congregations a sense of the "bigger church."

The Presbyterian Church has been, and continues to be, actively involved in the Meals on Wheels program.

SANTA MARIA PRESBYTERIAN CHURCH

AN ARTIST'S RENDERING OF THE PRESENT CHURCH FACILITY.
This, the third and present sanctuary, was constructed in 1961, and dedicated February 17, 1962.

SECOND BUILDING OF THE SANTA MARIA PRESBYTERIAN CHURCH
*This second facility, located at the corner of Cook and Lincoln, was constructed in 1911,
and was dedicated on March 13, 1913. Photograph courtsey of Jane Adam Drenon.*

BUILDING MODIFICATION TO SANTA MARIA PRESBYTERIAN CHURCH
*This photograph shows the design change and modifications to roof of the second facility
located at Cook and Lincoln.*

First Presbyterian Church — (1882-1911). Cor. Chapel & Vine St. (Photo courtesy Tommy Rice)

GOOD SAMARITAN SHELTER

The Presbyterians' Homeless Shelter had its beginnings January 31, 1986. Since that time, a facility has been constructed, and Santa Maria Presbyterian has been joined by various other churches, non-profit and civic organizations, as well as Marian Hospital, all of which contribute time and resources toward the operation of the facility.

CHAPTER THREE

FIRST CHRISTIAN CHURCH

EARLY HISTORY

In 1882, Reverend J. P. McCorkle, along with about 30 residents of the sparsely populated Central City, formed the Christian Church. The population of Central City was about 600 residents.

The first church building was on McClelland and Church Streets (at the current Mall location). These facilities served the church until 1953 when, overcrowded and condemned by the City of Santa Maria, they were forced to move to 200 South East Street.

The facilities at 200 South East Street were utilized for 37 years. In the 1980s, it became clear that new facilities would be needed. God provided the Rice Tract of land, and the church embarked on another adventure. The 200 South East Street church was purchased by the Vineyard Church in 1990.

The church currently sits upon 15.3 acres which were a part of the tract that now houses the Ford Dealership, Edwards Theater, and various other businesses.

The church moved into its current campus the first Sunday of December 1990. The first Sunday of December remains our Day of Rejoicing, celebrating the good gifts God has given us.

First Christian Church is now nondenominational.

A FRESH LOOK AT A VERY OLD CHURCH

You would never guess that First Christian is 129 years old (the third oldest church in Santa Maria). There is a youthful vitality that exists throughout the church. There are lots of programs and activities going on.

FCC ENGAGED

Engaging the people of First Christian Church with our community and our world is their mission. Their primary goal is community transformation. They also want to provide the people of First Christian Church with meaningful opportunities to live out their faith in their church, in their community, and in the world. These are not just "buzz words" -- read on!

FCC actively participated in helping Laurelglen Bible Church in Bakersfield build a 12' X 12' Loft house in Ensenada, Mexico. Panels for the pre-built house were cut and assembled on the church parking lot in Bakersfield, loaded on a trailer and later hauled to Ensenada where assembly and painting of the house took place.

In Santa Maria, First Christian Church joined forces with another church to build a fence and paint a house.

A tradition of several years at First Christian Church is to help ladies in the church who are widowed and single with car care.

CHILDREN'S SUNDAY MORNING PROGRAMS

FCC   is a very "kid friendly" place: There is a nursery for ages birth through 23 months; preschool for ages 2 years through kindergarten; elementary students grades 1 through 4; and Genesis - grades 5 and 6.

There are separate programs tailored for JUNIOR HIGH MINISTRY and HIGH SCHOOL MINISTRY.

MUSTARD SEED SINGLES MINISTRY (35+)

The Singles Ministry at FCC is committed to helping single adults "find and follow Christ" in their own lives, while also reaching out to others in service and fellowship.

SENIOR MINISTRY

There is a Senior Ministry called "Harbor Lights" for mature adults. Harbor Lights is involved in all areas of ministry at First Christian Church.

WORSHIP

There are two worship services every Sunday morning: 9:30 A.M. and 11:00 A.M.
Pastor: Clete Doyle

FIRST CHRISTIAN CHURCH
1550 South College Drive
Santa Maria, California
(805) 922-8479

FIRST CHRISTIAN CHURCH, SANTA MARIA, CALIFORNIA

This photograph of the congregation of the First Christian Church, located at McClelland and Church, was taken circa early 1900s, and was the first church building.

FIRST CHRISTIAN CHURCH SECOND BUILDING.
This, the second facility, located at 200 South East St., was constructed in 1953 and used until 1990.

STAINED GLASS WINDOWS REMOVED FROM SECOND CHURCH BUILDING.
Some of the stained glass windows from the second facility were removed and converted to window hangings for the present building, located at 1550 South College Drive.

CHURCH BELL MOVED TO NEW FACILITY.
The bell from the original facility was moved to the courtyard of the new campus following construction.

CHAPTER FOUR

ST. PETER'S EPISCOPAL CHURCH

EARLY HISTORY

June 28, 1897, marks the beginning of Episcopal presence in Santa Maria. The first service was conducted by Bishop Joseph Horsfall Johnson (1895-1928). The first service was conducted in the First Christian Church building on the corner of McClelland and Church Streets (which was later demolished to make way for the Mall). He was the first bishop of the Episcopal Diocese of Los Angeles. St. Peter's Parish is the northernmost parish in the diocese.

Episcopal services took place at various locations for quite a number of years, as they had no church building of their own. During the summer of 1913, the Right Reverend G. Mott Williams, Bishop of Marquette, Michigan, was involved in a serious accident while driving over San Marcos Pass. He was brought to Santa Maria for hospitalization and recuperative treatment. His attending physician was Dr. Robert Brown, a parish member. During his convalescence, Bishop Williams developed a keen interest in St. Peter's and was troubled by the lack of a church structure.

When Dr. Brown refused payment for his treatment, Bishop Williams collected $90.00 in insurance money and gave it to Dr. Brown as the beginning of the St. Peter's building fund. Six years later, with help from the Women's Guild, a Guild Hall was built at 402 South Lincoln, where they are today.

The Guild Hall stood on the east end of the lot with its entrance facing north on Cook Street until 1932, when it was moved to the southwest corner of the lot.

On September 24, 1932, the cornerstone was placed for the sanctuary building at 402 South Lincoln Street, and the opening service was held on December 24, 1932.

St. Peter's Mission voted to become a parish on January 13, 1947.

The entrance to the church was moved in 1960 from Lincoln Street to the south side of the building, opening to the courtyard. The Parish Hall was built in 1959.

The church is a charming Old English style building with a wooden spire. The wooden spire is topped with a cross, upon which sits a rooster. The rooster is associated with St. Peter's denial of Christ on the day he was crucified, and has become a symbol of the forgiveness of God.

The building was erected in 1932 and has a seating capacity of 140.

There are 55 stained glass windows present in the nave and sanctuary. Most were the work of Judson Studios in Pasadena, California. The eldest of them date from the 1930s and the latest were completed as part of a massive renovation of the church completed in 2011.

MORE RECENT HISTORY, MINISTRIES, AND OUTREACH

Good Samaritan Shelter:

Members of St. Peter's have been volunteering time, food, and money to the local homeless facility (the Good Samaritan Shelter) for the past 20 years. Volunteers from St. Peter's prepare and serve 110-140 dinners and sack lunches at the shelter on the third Wednesday of each month.

Martha's Meals:

On June 5, 2009, the Martha's Meals Program received a grant from the Marian Outreach Fund. Additionally, an anonymous donation was made to the program. The ministry began informally in 2007 with the purchase of food cards from Jack in the Box. In 2008 and 2009, it evolved into putting together nutritious, economical, shelf stable bag lunches, allowing the church to feed more individuals and families. Requests for assistance soon increased from 6-8 per week to over 25 per day. It is expected that requests may continue to increase due in large part to the economic downturn. In addition to the daily sack lunches, each Thursday morning the program distributes about 50 bags of groceries to the working poor. We have been encouraged by the assistance of the Methodist Church and participation by volunteers from the community outside of St. Peter's. This program was always meant to grow beyond the bounds of St. Peter's to tend the needs of the people trying to survive in the center of the city.

RagDolls2Love:

Soft, colorful, pancake style rag dolls are created for children who are enduring trauma or stress in their lives. During Lent 2009, 135 rag dolls were made with the help of the youth from the church. On the Sunday after Easter, the sanctuary was filled with dolls of all colors and patterns. Parishioners gathered the dolls and took them to the altar to be blessed before being sent to Marian Medical Center for use in the ER, Pediatrics and out-patient surgery. These huggable dolls are created at a workshop held the first Thursday of each month throughout the year.

Easter Baskets:

Food-filled Easter baskets are provided to the Salvation Army for distribution to needy families in our community by a committee from St. Peter's.

Many churches and organizations provide food baskets at Thanksgiving and Christmas; therefore St. Peter's decided to reach out to those in need at Easter.

Red Shirt Project:

Deborah Dunn, St. Peter's rector, Michael Cunningham, rector of St. Mary's in Lompoc, and the Rev. Robert Two Bulls, Director of Indian Work for the Diocese of Minnesota have spent the last eleven years leading the journeys of young people from the Diocese of Los Angeles to Red Shirt, South Dakota on the Pine Ridge Reservation. Rev. Two Bulls is a member of the Oglala Lakota tribe and a second generation Episcopal priest. This reservation is listed by the Bureau of Indian Affairs as the poorest in the United States.

Every year participants, including youths and adults from several churches, worked on various building projects across the reservation and helped to lead a Vacation Bible Study program at Christ Episcopal Church in Red Shirt. St. Peter's supports this ministry with annual donations.

St. Peter's Episcopal Church
402 Lincoln Street
Santa Maria, California 93458
PH: (805) 922-3575

The Reverend Canon Deborah Dunn, Rector
The Reverend Faye Hogan, Pastoral Associate

Sunday Services:
8:00 a.m. and 11:00 a.m. Holy Communion
Every fourth Sunday there is an additional service at 5:00 p.m.

Wednesday Service at 10:00 a.m.
Holy Communion and Healing Prayer

ALL PHOTOGRAPHY FOR THIS CHAPTER WAS PROVIDED BY KIRK IRWIN

ST. PETER'S EPISCOPAL CHURCH, SANTA MARIA, CALIFORNIA

ST. PETER'S EPISCOPAL CHURCH.
Rededication Services of the Renovated Sanctuary, November 2010.

Photograph courtesy of Kirk Irwin

ST. PETER'S EPISCOPAL CHURCH.
Easter Services, 2011.

Photograph courtesy of Kirk Irwin

CHAPTER FIVE

THE SALVATION ARMY

INTRODUCTION: WILLIAM BOOTH, A MAN WHOSE VISION CHANGED THE WORLD

To fully appreciate The Salvation Army in Santa Maria, California, it is important to understand the history of how the organization came into existence.

In 1865 in London, England, William Booth, an ordained Methodist minister aided by his wife Catherine, formed an evangelical group dedicated to preaching among the "unchurched" people living in the midst of appalling poverty in London's East End.

Booth's ministry recognized the interdependence of material, emotional and spiritual needs. In addition to preaching the gospel of Jesus Christ, Booth became involved in feeding and shelter of the hungry and homeless, and in rehabilitation of alcoholics. Booth pressed the Methodist church to open its eyes to the surrounding poverty. The Booths were pressured to resign from the Methodist church.

Booth formed his own Christian mission and started out preaching in a tent. He and his followers, originally known as The Christian Mission, became The Salvation Army in 1878 when that organization evolved on a quasi-military pattern. Booth became "the General", and officers' ranks were given to his ministers. This organizational structure still exists today.

Currently, The Salvation Army exists in 124 different countries, and continues to spread the word of God and promote Christian ideals. It has evolved over the decades into a social service provider with an unmatched scope and breadth.

EVOLUTION OF THE SALVATION ARMY KETTLES

In December of 1891, a Salvation Army Captain in San Francisco had resolved to provide a free Christmas dinner to the area's poor. But how would he pay for the food?

As he went about his daily tasks, the question stayed in his mind. Suddenly his thoughts went back to his days as a sailor in Liverpool, England. On the Stage Landing he had seen a large pot called "Simpson's pot", into which charitable donations were thrown by passers-by.

The next morning he secured permission from the authorities to place a similar pot at the Oakland ferry landing at the foot of Market Street. No time was lost in securing a pot and placing it in a conspicuous position, so it could be seen by all those going to and from the ferry boats. In addition, a brass urn was placed on a stand in the waiting room for the same purpose.

Thus, Captain Joseph McFee launched a tradition that has spread not only throughout the United States, but throughout the world.   It still continues today.

SOLDIERS WITHOUT SWORDS

During William Booth's lifetime, he vigorously denied that the Salvation Army was a "denomination."   A few months after the United States entered World War I, in September 1917, a declaration by the Judge Advocate General of the War Department, that the Salvation Army was indeed a religious denomination, was welcomed.   Salvation Army Officers became eligible for service as Chaplains.

General John J. Pershing granted permission for the Salvation Army to establish a ministry in France.   Pershing ordered the Salvationists into regulation khaki-colored privates uniforms, with the red Salvation Army shield on caps and epaulettes.

The YMCA was already chartered by the Government in France, but the Salvation Army brought many wonderful "touches of home" to the American military troops there.

THE DONUT GIRLS

The rations of the American Expeditionary Forces were very limited.   Four Salvation Army "lassies" with the American First Division wondered what they could do to supplement the chocolate bars in their canteens.   Ensign Margaret Sheldon suggested, "Why not make donuts?"   Flour and lard were secured, but because the girls had no rolling pin the dough was patted into shape.   The top of a baking powder can served to cut out the donuts and a camphor ice tube to cut out the holes.   The first donut was fried by Adjutant Helen Purviance, and the first batch was an immediate hit with the soldiers.

Although the donut became the symbol of the Salvation Army in France, pies and cakes were also baked by the girls in crude ovens, and lemonade was served to hot and thirsty troops as well.

A special correspondent of the New York Times wrote under the heading, "With the American Army in France":   "When I landed in France I didn't think so much of the Salvation Army; after two weeks with the Americans at the front I take off my hat to the Salvation Army.   And when the memoirs of this war come to be written the donuts and apple pies of the Salvation Army are going to take their place in history."

SANTA MARIA CORPS HISTORY

Santa Maria's Salvation Army began March 1, 1898, with Captain J. Hansen assigned as its first minister.

Early historical records are minimal -- a few old newspaper clippings, etc. The Salvation Army was more into DOING what they were founded for and not into documenting what they had DONE. Like the Energizer bunny, they just kept going and going from March 1, 1898 forward!

An article written and published October 22, 1977, by the United Way provides insight and depicts the enormous impact on early Santa Maria:

> "The Salvation Army, motivated by love for God and a practical concern for the needs of humanity, has established a diversified program of religious and social welfare services designed to meet the needs of children, youth, and adults -- people of all ages.

> "Included in its year-round program is the welfare emergency relief fund that assists transients, transient and resident families in food, lodging or transportation.

> "There are community clubs for both men and women in which there is opportunity for individuals to have fun and friendship. There are also new programs to be begun that includes boys and girls recreational clubs with activities and outings.

> "Summer brings about the day camp season of which there are four weeks of day camp activities. This day camp is unique in that it is the only day camp in the community that is of no cost to the child and, at the same time, gives that child a good hot lunch. It is hoped in the future to reach more youngsters by increasing the number of children that is permitted every week for day camp.

> "The winter programs include the Salvation Army's annual Christmas effort. The Vandenberg Air Force Base "Big Brother" operation reaches out to more than 100 - 150 youngsters from referrals through the Salvation Army. Along with working together with the local Air Force base during Christmas, there is also the giving of food baskets and visits to hospital patients in different institutions throughout the community.

> "The Salvation Army of Santa Maria looks forward towards increasing its service to more individuals in the future than the 12,000 persons seeking help in 1976. This will be possible for the Salvation Army to do so because of the local community support. It is because of this sincere and compassionate support that this Salvation Army survives; and it would be impossible for us to accomplish the things stated without the local United Way organization."

The following photograph, with an accompanying article, was published in December 1991 by the *Santa Maria Times*, and describes one of the Salvation Army's many programs with local schools.

Student generosity

Times/Scott Wheeler

Students in Linda Ford's seventh- and eighth-grade social studies classes at Fesler Junior High School show off the toys they purchased to donate to the Salvation Army's Secret Santa program. The students collected $200 to buy the toys. They also made decorations for the Salvation Army's Thanksgiving dinner.

The Salvation Army serves lunches at noon Monday through Friday at their facility located at 402 South Miller Street in Santa Maria. Church services are conducted every Sunday at that same location. Lts. Paul & Jennifer Swain are the officers. And on June 6th, the stork delivered a little lieutenant by the name of Benjamin! Then on June 29, 2011, two additional Lieutenants, Matthew Richard Jensen and Vanessa Jensen were appointed to Santa Maria. They have a 2-½ year old daughter, Brooke Rose. Both of the Jensens graduated from Seminary on June 12, 2011. Welcome to Santa Maria.

In recent years, the "politically correct" crowd has influenced some businesses to not allow the Salvation Army to have their kettles outside their establishments during Thanksgiving and Christmas holidays. Other businesses continued to WELCOME them.

These humble servants toil in our midst on a daily basis just as they have for more than 113 years in the Santa Maria Valley. They nourish the bodies as well as the souls of those most in need. Thanks to individual donors and the help of corporate partners, they feed the hungry 365 days a year.

The mission statement of the Salvation Army is:

DOING THE MOST GOOD

CHAPTER SIX

ST. MARY OF THE ASSUMPTION
ROMAN CATHOLIC CHURCH

Around the turn of the, century, the Catholic families living in Santa Maria had to travel to Guadalupe, Sisquoc, or Arroyo Grande to attend Mass. The priests who made the 40-mile trek from Santa Inez to Santa Maria to make sick calls, baptize babies, perform marriages, and to occasionally conduct services in private homes, knew that the time had come for Santa Maria to have a church of its own.

The Reverend John McNally was responsible for the building of the Mission of San Isador, (now "Our Lady of Guadalupe Church") in Guadalupe in 1875, as well as the chapel dedicated as "The San Ramon Chapel" in 1879. Since both chapels were located a sizeable distance from Santa Maria, the town's Catholics (75 families) wanted and needed a church of their own, complete with a resident priest.

On August 20, 1905, the Holy Sacrifice of the Mass was celebrated for the first time for the Catholic families in Santa Maria by the Reverend Mathias Ternes at McMillan's Hall (the opera house). The Reverend Ternes, who had been ordained in Rome on October 31, 1902, and appointed first rector to St. Mary of the Assumption by Bishop Thomas J. Conaty of Los Angeles, gave a rousing sermon that day about the needs of the parish. However, that was only the beginning.

Two weeks later, after the Reverend Ternes rented the old Methodist Church building, the first Mass in the building was celebrated and continued to be used as a place of worship for the area's Catholics until a church of their own could be built.

ST. MARY OF THE ASSUMPTION CHURCH.
Dedication of St. Mary's first church building was on February 11, 1906.

In less than a month, so generous were the donations and subscriptions, that Father Ternes felt that enough funds had been pledged to begin construction of a parish residence. A few days after Father Ternes moved into the rectory on December 26, 1905, construction began at the corner of Cypress and Miller Streets on a brick veneer church with a seating capacity of four hundred.

Dedication of the first Catholic church building took place on February 11, 1906.

Through the years, the Reverend Ternes made many friends and converts and did much to promote good feelings toward the church. When the Reverend Cohen was serving as pastor, and the heavy rains caused the area to be inundated with water, leaving the unpaved streets in a sad state of disrepair, he appealed to the city for help. However, the city fathers didn't see things his way, and turned him down. Without further ado, the good Father borrowed a plow and grader, rolled up his sleeves and fixed the streets himself!

Well-remembered is Father Dubbel, St. Mary's pastor during the First World War. A forceful and vigorous man, he made many converts and was instrumental in thwarting the budding KKK organizations in the district during those years. Due in great part to his efforts, they were never able to get a real foothold in the community.

Next came Fr. Albert Hurley, who was one of the most popular pastors of Santa Maria.

When the Rev. Thomas V. Murphy, an Irishman who fell in love with his adopted country, became pastor of St. Mary's on August 10, 1933, the only buildings standing were the church and the rectory. By September of 1938, with only a $20,000 note against them, a parochial school and convent, housing the Sisters of St. Francis of Penance and Christian Charity, were standing ready to serve the community. By 1948, a $40,000 addition to the school was built, and another $40,000 piece of property stood across the street from the church. In 1951, the Convent was enlarged to provide for the additional teachers needed in the growing school.

Since the Sisters of St. Francis were already staffing St. Mary's School, Monsignor Murphy requested that Sisters from the same order establish a hospital in Santa Maria. On November 22, 1939, ground was broken for the 35-bed facility located at 125 Airport Avenue (now College Drive).

The hospital, now located on the 10 acres of land donated by Captain and Mrs. Allan Hancock, and known as the Marian Medical Center, has a reputation in the medical care field as being second to none.

As the years passed, and with over 2,000 Catholic families in town, the need for a later church became apparent. In 1957, plans were drawn up by Architect George J. Adams, and Doane Construction Company was contracted to build a new church to seat approximately 1,000 people.

Also included were plans for a new two-story rectory.   When the first Mass was celebrated in the new church on September 14, 1958,   bells of the old St. Mary's Church, which had been placed in the 100-foot tower of the new church, rang out to welcome the parishioners to Mass. His Eminence, Cardinal McIntyre on March 15, 1959, dedicated the new church.

St. Mary of the Assumption Church stood in service to the entire community until Cardinal McIntyre, seeing the ever-increasing growth in the Santa Maria and Orcutt area, felt that the needs of the community would be better met if the area were split into two parts.

St. Louis de Montfort parish was created in March of 1963 to ease the situation and meet the needs of the people in the southern part of Santa Maria and Orcutt.

July 1964, Father Kieran Marum was appointed to St. Mary's to serve as administrator under Msgr. Murphy. Msgr. Marum was ordained on June 19, 1943, in St. Patrick's Seminary in Maynooth, Dublin, Ireland. He arrived in Los Angeles in 1948, where he taught high school and had parish assignments before coming to St. Mary's of the Assumption.

On February 6, 1966, open house was held in the new Parish Hall, which had been constructed on the site of the former church on the corner of Miller and Cypress Streets. However, the building didn't stop there.

In January 1968, the two houses west of the rectory on East Church Street, a duplex on South Miller (now Msgr. Colberg's home), as well as three garages were donated to St. Mary's Church by Maria J. Vicente.

PRESENT ST. MARY'S CHURCH BUILDING.
The first Mass was celebrated in the new church on September 14, 1958

On April 27, 1973, the first Mass and blessing of the newly constructed Parish Center on West Orchard Street was held (now St. John Neumann's Parish Hall). This multipurpose hall was built, not only to serve as a place in which to hold Mass, but to hold CCD classes several times a week as well.

In 1974 Msgr. Marum was reassigned to St. Finabar's in Burbank. Msgr. Colberg was appointed in his place as the pastor, serving until his retirement in 1999, when Fr. Riz Carranza was appointed to lead the people of St. Mary's into the new millennium.

Long gone are the days when a priest from Santa Inez made periodic trips into Santa Maria to perform religious services for the little settlement of Catholics. Even though St. Louis de Montfort and St. John Neumann Churches eased the crowded conditions of St. Mary's, the number of parishioners represented by the many different cultures continues to grow.

ST. MARY'S SCHOOL

The following article, provided by St. Mary of the Assumption Church, describes the beginnings and development of St. Mary of the Assumption School in Santa Maria since 1938.

Santa Maria

Saint Mary of the Assumption

Santa Maria was a small agricultural community with a population of 8,000 when excavations began for St. Mary of the Assumption School on June 17, 1938. Construction was completed in record time and regular classes began on September 14. Fifty-nine students were enrolled in grades one through eight under the guidance of the Franciscan Sisters of Penance and Christian Charity. On June 16, 1939, six eighth graders – three boys and three girls – became St. Mary of the Assumption's charter class.

The original building at St. Mary consisted of a four-room unit; two grades shared a single classroom. This arrangement lasted until 1948 when construction of a second four-classroom unit was begun. At the same time, the parish also purchased the property across Cypress Street from the church, which was subsequently fenced in for the main playground. In 1960-1961 and again in 1963-1964 two more four-room units were added. By September 1964 St. Mary of the Assumption was a double grade school.

Growth at St. Mary of the Assumption during the ensuing years was steady but slow. By 1971, however, the presence of another parochial school in Santa Maria coupled with archdiocesan policy dictated the gradual elimination of double grades. The "phase-out" was completed by 1975-1976. A kindergarten was opened in 1985.

CHAPTER SEVEN

ORCUTT PRESBYTERIAN CHURCH

EARLY HISTORY

The history of the Orcutt Presbyterian Church, founded in 1907, really began in 1901. W.W. Orcutt, chief geologist for the Union Oil Company, set about to locate oil fields and tirelessly explored large tracts of land.

Orcutt traveled by buckboard, spring wagon, on horseback or on foot. He confidently laid out a town to serve as a supply base in what he felt would someday be a massive oil field. In 1904, when highly productive wells like Old Maud came in, the Black Gold Rush was on, and the people rush began.

Where the people were, God was present. The Rev. Sloan of the Bible Institute came in his chuck wagon church home to preach the gospel of Jesus Christ.

Later the Newlove School House and the Grasciosa boarding house served as church building and Sunday School for those living on the hill. One of the Union Oil Company surveyors, Mr. William Ferguson, suggested a plot of land in Orcutt be set aside for a church.

The original plot was located on Pinal Street.   However, when it came time to build, the plot was traded for the location at the corner of Union Avenue and Pacific Street.

The Orcutt Community Church building was completed in 1907 on the corner of Union and Pacific, financed by the townspeople and the Union Oil Company.   The pews were brought from a church in Guadalupe and were used until 1947, at which time they were replaced.   The building was used as a school in 1922 with Miss May Grisham as the teacher.

For a time, the Methodist Episcopalians were the sponsoring group for the church.

About 1916, Rev. W.F.S. Nelson, pastor of the First Presbyterian Church in Santa Maria, was authorized by the Santa Barbara Presbytery to preach at several points throughout the oil fields.   He was called the "Sky Pilot", and traveled by horse and buggy with his small portable organ, preaching in Pismo Beach, Nipomo, Sisquoc, Guadalupe, Betteravia, Casmalia, Los Alamos and the oil leases Graciosa, Newlove Hill and Bicknell.

Around 1938, the Santa Barbara Presbytery sent several student ministers from San Anselmo to preach in Orcutt and in Los Alamos on weekends.   They also spent their summer vacations in this area, helping in the church work.   Two of the student ministers were Ellis Marshburn and Melvin Nelson.   Mr. Nelson was with the church for a year, and was instrumental in preparing the congregations of Los Alamos and Orcutt for organization under the Presbyterian Mission Board.

Rev. Phillip Lascelles, 1941-1947

The first resident pastor, Rev. Phillip Lascelles, organized the church with 35 members on January 13, 1941.   The budget for that year was $500.   Los Alamos was part of the parish. Orcutt did not receive help from the Presbyterian National Board of Missions until 1944.

Rev. Ross Linsenmayer, 1947-1951

Rev. and Mrs Ross Linsenmayer came to serve the church in 1947 and were able to give it new impetus.   They led an effort to transform the ugly surroundings into a place of beauty.

During Rev. Linsenmayer's tenure, the Youth Cabin, also known as the Camp Fire Cabin, was moved from Orcutt School property, with the agreement that the Camp Fire Girls would have a meeting place.

Growth in the Santa Maria Valley

With the advent of the missile age in the 1950s, the Air Force recommended the transfer of Camp Cooke from the Army for use as a missile training base.   Its remote location and proximity to the coast offered a perfect setting for safely launching intermediate range ballistic missiles and intercontinental ballistic missiles to targets in the Pacific Ocean. These same geographic features were also ideal for launching satellites into polar orbit, without overflight of populated land masses during missile liftoff.

On October 4, 1958, Cooke AFB was renamed Vandenberg AFB in honor of the late General Hoyt S. Vandenberg, the Air Force's second Chief of Staff. With Vandenberg AFB on the drawing board, new challenges needed to be met as the unbelievable projected growth of the community commenced.

With the tremendous growth in the Santa Maria Valley came the need to build a new church building. On December 8, 1963, a new building was dedicated at 993 Patterson Road and is still home to Orcutt Presbyterian Church today.

MEALS ON WHEELS

Meals on wheels was first organized in the Santa Maria Valley by Bob Wedaa. Rev. Robert Wedaa was the pastor from 1969-1994. There was no money from the government and meals were delivered by volunteers, many from the church. Bob recalled that meals were regularly delivered to a gentleman who lived in a hotel on North Broadway. To all appearances he had no money or other resources. However, upon his death, $35,000 was left to the Meals on Wheels program by this man!

Many outreach programs to the community were commenced by the church in the late 1970s and continue to this day.

ORCUTT PRESBYTERIAN CHURCH
993 Patterson Road
Santa Maria, CA   93455
(805) 937-4974
Pastor: Rev. Bruce Lethbridge

CHAPTER EIGHT

SEVENTH-DAY ADVENTIST

EARLY HISTORY

Although there is evidence to show that there were Seventh-day Adventists in the Santa Maria area as far back as 1880, there was no organized church established until May 14, 1932. The first Seventh-day Adventist family appears to have been the McElhanys who had a country home on the outskirts of Santa Maria.

Yearning for Christian education for their children, the McElhany family bid farewell to their business at McElhany Hall in Santa Maria, and the year 1887 found Father McElhany, and his children, enrolled in Healdsburg Academy, near St. Helena, California. Serious minded James Lamar McElhany, Jr. later became president of the General Conference of Seventh-day Adventists.

Cottage meetings continued in Santa Maria and more Christian lights continued to shine. Fellow believers in Santa Maria and Arroyo Grande assisted E. Torel Seat and singing evangelist R. D. Moon in a tent meeting at East Church and South McClelland in 1931. Arthur Escobar and 89 others were baptized, and meetings continued in the Odd Fellow's Hall on Broadway Avenue.

May 14, 1932, the church family organized the first Santa Maria Seventh-day Adventist Church. Clark Adams was the first minister. Two lots were purchased at 210 West Fesler; a building was torn down and church building construction began. Samuel Grigg, E. Torel Seat and his father were the principal builders. All members had a part, utilizing used lumber and straightening nails. The arched windows had green, purple and gold stained glass. In front of the sanctuary, two eight-foot brown boards bore gold leaf writing of the Ten Commandments. Two Sabbath School rooms were soon filled with the singing voices of children. A belfry, containing the bell from the Washington Country School, was later torn down. A small building behind the church was often rented or used for storage. The second lot was sold.

A Dorcas society was organized to help the needy of the community and disaster areas. As they sewed each week, they always had a devotional and often read the promise in Psalm 41:1 and 2, "Blessed is he who considers the poor . . . . The Lord protects him and keeps him alive."

In 1934 members began planning for a church school, and the following year the school opened in the south room of the church. The teacher's salary was $55.00 a month, and Teacher Toews stayed at one home and ate at another, and at one time lived in one corner of the classroom, paying part of the utilities. When the attendance grew to need two classrooms, one teacher donated her time for two years. In 1957, the school was held at the Spanish-speaking Seventh-day Adventist Church.

When the freeway was completed in 1958, a school bus was rented and students were bused to Arroyo Grande. Funds were raised to buy buses and to build two new classrooms, and in 1961 a ten-grade school was established. More funds were needed to build an auditorium-classroom complex, and the school was named Valley View Junior Academy.

Arthur Escobar was the first missionary volunteer leader and choir director. Max Sibayan taught him how to pray.

Many colporteurs, spreading the printed word like fallen leaves, have spent many hours in Santa Maria.

Each pastor and a number of evangelists have held series of meetings proclaiming the love of Jesus and His certain return. In 1946, Elder Robert E. Reynolds, calling his tent the Bible Auditorium, had meetings in Orcutt. Elder Mead McGuire held meetings in the church, touching many hearts. Elders Stanley Harris and William Hoffman held two different lecture series at the Santa Barbara County Fairgrounds.

Elders Richard Rentfro, Duane Corwin and Jerry Dill also held meetings in the area.

In 1957, around $4,000 was spent to redecorate the church. The squeaky theater seats, with hat racks under each one, were removed, and oak pews and platform furniture were installed. Two coats of paint were needed, inside and out, and the pastor encouraged the members to paint every three years, so they could always enjoy each coat of paint.

A small building was torn down and a Dorcas society/classroom addition was added to the church in 1961, but the congregation began to outgrow the sanctuary. In 1963, the Pacific Union Conference officials reviewed the Santa Maria church members' financial capabilities and recommended the 210 West Fesler property be sold for approximately $30,000, and raise $17,000 for the Valley View School. It was also suggested they spend $15,000 for a lot and build a $68,000 church. In March of 1964, members pledged to raise $54,000 in three years. With God's help, they were beginning a seemingly impossible task.

Manfred Sanders gave 2.6 acres of land at 1775 South Thornburg upon which to build a church. This gave immeasurable courage to the members. The next week the young people's meeting was held in the ditch of the property. Hymns of praise were sung, accompanied by a clarinet and a flute.

Elder R. R. Breitigam, chairman of the Santa Barbara church building committee, came in 1965 to advise. Plans were drawn for Phase I, including a multipurpose room, kitchen, and three classrooms, with a community service area in the front of the building.

On October 1, 1967, the Mayor, charter member Martha Friday, and Amy Foland, oldest member, assisted in the groundbreaking, with golden shovels. Building chairman Charles Redell and Pastor Richard Minesinger officiated.

MOVING FORWARD – MORE CURRENT HISTORY AND ACTIVITIES

Adventist Schools:

Valley View Adventist Academy
The Valley View Adventist Academy in Arroyo Grande   is still going strong in spite of the downturn in the economy. This school is for Kindergarten up to Grade 10. VVAA's Principal is Philip Ermshar. There are hot lunch and extended-care programs. VVAA has a 50/50 matching scholarship program when   possible.   Kindergarten space is available for the 2011-2012 school year.

Monterey Bay Academy
The Monterey Bay Academy is a Boarding Academy in Selva Beach, California, (near Watsonville) for Central California.   Students are grades freshmen through seniors.

Outreach Activities:

The Seventh-day Adventist Church has many ongoing outreach activities in Santa Maria. They have just concluded the summer program of participation in PICNIC IN THE PARK. This was a program of food distribution in the parks during the summer.   They also had a Vacation Bible School.

Prison Ministries – Visitation, Bible studies, baptisms

Summer Camp – Located in Yosemite Park, Wawona. Our five students went in July. One week sessions with various activities, learning about Jesus and the outdoors.

Camp Meeting – Also held in July for 10 days; held in the Soquel Campgrounds in Central California.

The church is part of an outreach ministry to both Villa Maria and Country Oaks, where they share songs, scriptures, poems and special music. LeRoy and Jackie Jones coordinate this function.

Lest you think the "mature" crowd is left out, there is a 50+ CLUB. This group gets together for various activities, including going out to eat together on occasion.

On July 2, 2011, the Seventh-day Adventist Church had a special event take place: Michael Harris, who does MINISTRY IN SONG all over the world, blessed the congregation with his golden voice.   Pastor Jose Vazquez was out of the area that Saturday.

This church has succeeded in blending all ethnic groups into one well-organized "family." There are English groups, Spanish groups, and Filipino groups all meeting for lesson studies in different sections of the sanctuary, then all coming together for worship service at the same time.   Quite an accomplishment!

ROSTER OF CHURCH LEADERS

Pastor Jose Vazquez
Head Elder, LeRoy Jones
Clerk, Helen Parker
Head Deacon, Richard Perez
Head Deaconess, Shirley Drake
Treasurer, Jason Schellas
Bulletin Secretary, Georgia Schellas
Valley View Adventist Academy Principal, Philip E. Ermshar

SANTA MARIA SEVENTH-DAY ADVENTIST CHURCH
1775 South Thornburg Street
Santa Maria, California   93458

EVERYTHING WE DO WITH ACTIVITIES AND OUTREACH PROJECTS IS FOR THE GLORY OF GOD, WINNING SOULS FOR JESUS AND ASSISTING PEOPLE BY OUTREACHING TO THOSE IN NEED IN OUR COMMUNITY.

CHAPTER NINE

FOURSQUARE CHURCH

EARLY HISTORY

To better understand the Foursquare Church, a word about its founder is in order. It was started by Amie Kennedy Simple McPherson in the 1920s in a tent in Los Angeles. It was incorporated in 1927 as a Pentecostal church.

Although not formally organized in Santa Maria until June 26, 1928, the Foursquare ministry actually began in July 1927, when four LIFE Bible College students journeyed from Los Angeles to Santa Maria in their Model "T" coupes. The students held a 10-day revival in the Princess Theatre on Pine Street.

One of the musicians from Angelus Temple who performed at the revival, Peggy King, returned to Santa Maria to work with the local people on establishing a church. The first meeting place of the group was at the Orcutt Ladies Club House.

Peggy King and Stella Allcot of Santa Maria, referred to as "The Girls", toured the oil fields, inviting oil workers to attend meetings. The girls rented an apartment above the Orcutt Mercantile Store. Mr. Righetti offered an old saloon building, rent free, next to the pool hall in which to hold meetings.

After the formation of a church on June 26, 1928, the search began for a more suitable meeting place. Some of the sites used included the Orcutt library building and even a butcher shop building.

PRESENT-DAY FOURSQUARE CHURCH
SANCTUARY

Finally, the congregation moved into Santa Maria and rented the old Methodist Church building on the northwest corner of Church and Lincoln Streets, which was utilized until their first building was completed.

In 1929, property was purchased on the northeast corner of Curryer and Fesler Streets. The first church building was erected at a total cost of $4,500. This church building was utilized until 1959, when a new church building was erected at the corner of Curryer and Hermosa Streets.

Need for a new and expanded church facility became evident in 1977. The church elected to remain at its same location, rebuilding and expanding.

On Easter Sunday, 1978, the first worship service was held in the new and expanded sanctuary.

ONGOING AND CURRENT PROGRAMS AND ACTIVITIES

Senior Pastors, Roger and Janet Wheeler, have been overseeing the ministry of the Santa Maria Foursquare Church for the past 23 years. They have experienced many blessings with the congregation during that season, and they have planted a number of churches with pastors and leaders, who have been trained at the local facility and then "sent out" with a prayer covering. In 2004 and 2005, the Santa Maria Church "blessed out" two congregations to the Central Coast: the "New Beginnings Foursquare Church", pastored by Larry and Maria Tajon (on McCoy Street in Santa Maria); and "Shouts of Grace", located in the 5-Cities Area, and pastored by Pat and Terry Sparrow.

The next year they "blessed out" the Spanish congregation of Iglesia Internacional Casa de Dios, pastored by Ricardo Herrera. In 2006, the Santa Maria Church also sent out their Associate Pastor and his wife, Ron and Debra Brown, to pioneer a Foursquare Church in Christchurch, New Zealand. The Browns soon became the Foursquare supervising overseers for the entire country of New Zealand, and are currently stationed in Auckland.

The Foursquare Church in Santa Maria has been very committed to a "Discipleship Model" of ministry that is designed to "raise up" leaders (not just practicing Christians—but fully equipped and "disciple" leaders) for the work of ministry, according to the Biblical criteria.

The church has also been committed to the "fellowship of the saints" with the body of Christ. Pastor Wheeler has been an active member, and a former President, of the Santa Maria Ministerial Association, which is very involved in the community and reaches out to many churches and even non-Christians, with the message of the Gospel of Christ.

For 24 years, the Foursquare Church also operated an Elementary School for Kindergarten through the 6th Grade. It closed in 2004, but the Christian Life Preschool has continued to operate in the community to the present time. The Pre-school Director is Cynthia Sustiata.

CHRISTIAN LIFE PRESCHOOL

The Santa Maria Foursquare Church started a "U-Turn" program designed to reach Junior High and Senior High School young people. They pioneered a number of projects and facility enhancements to communicate to the youth their importance to God and the community. The Youth Pastor, Gabe Dominguez, leads this program.

Reaching out to the community, from the years 2000-2005, and funded by the church and grants from the county, state and federal level, the "Foursquare Youth Programs," offering four specific areas of training and education included: Jobs to Career; Mentoring; Skills for Success; and Making Families First.

The Santa Maria Foursquare Church has also been offering a Celebrate Recovery Program on a weekly basis, designed to help people struggling with hurts, hang-ups, and habits, by showing them the loving power of Jesus Christ through the recovery process.

In recent years, the church has also developed a number of small groups, meeting weekly, to help people of all ages and ethnic backgrounds deal with the moral and spiritual problems that confront our society.

Rescue Mission: Two nights a week the Rescue Mission serves a hot meal to anyone in need in the gymnasium.

Tree of Life Ministries: This is a program for children, birth through 6th grade.

Kingdom Kids: This program is for Kindergarten and 1st grades.

The Associate Pastor of Foursquare Church is Dennis Jordan.   The Worship Pastors are Dr. Merkel and Theresa Quareles.   The Children's Pastor is Tonya Williams.

For more than 20 years, the Santa Maria Foursquare Church has also offered a ministry for Spanish-speaking individuals.   The church, overall, is made up of people of all racial and ethnic backgrounds, with the congregation currently reflecting the culture and ethnicity of the community of Santa Maria. The Spanish Pastors are Joel and Veronica Arreola.

FOURSQUARE CHURCH
709 North Curryer
Santa Maria, California 93458
Website: www.santamariafoursquare.com

CHAPTER TEN

CHRIST UNITED METHODIST CHURCH

By the early 1900s, the Santa Maria Valley had become an important farming area. Significant numbers of Japanese immigrants came, mostly to work in agriculture. By the 1920s there were about 1000 Japanese people in the Santa Maria area, and some of them were Christians. In January of 1927, a Japanese Christian following was formed under the leadership of Saika and Kuramoto families. It was named the "Friends of Jesus". The fellowship was assisted by two Japanese ministers, Rev. Otoe So and Rev. Nisato, who were able to occasionally come to Santa Maria. In August of 1928, a Sunday School was started. After a few months, an old schoolhouse on Guadalupe Road (now West Main) was secured. That building became the "church" for the Japanese Christians in our area.

With the groundwork already laid, the boards of home missions of the Congregational, Presbyterian, Methodist and Christian churches joined together to support the establishment of a Japanese Christian Mission in Santa Maria. A visitation evangelist, Mrs. Kane Yajima, was sent here to help get things started. She stayed for six months until a permanent pastor was found.

CHRIST UNITED METHODIST CHURCH.
Construction on the church building was completed on September 16, 1937,
just eight years after the founding of the church, and is still in use today

On September 16, 1929, the "Japanese Union Church of Santa Maria" was founded. Rev. Yasuo Oshita was named its Pastor. There were 7 charter members: Shichizo Saika,

Hanaye Saika, Totaro Utsunomiya, Toyo Utsunomiya, Tamego Mori, Isu Mori, and Nobuko Ito (The Kuramotos had earlier moved to the Imperial Valley).

In the early years, the church grew rapidly, and by 1934, serious planning and fund raising for a permanent church building were in progress. Those efforts culminated in the completion of the church building on September 16, 1937, just eight years after the founding of the church. That building has stood the test of time, and is still our church home (219 Mary Drive, Santa Maria).

On October 3, 1937, a beautiful worship service and church building dedication ceremony was held with as many as 500 members and friends attending. The records seem to indicate that when the building was completed, there was no outstanding debt.

There were two people attending the 80th Anniversary Celebration (October 2009) who were involved in the 1937 building dedication service: Aiko Uyeno, nee Shintani was baptized that day, and Mrs. Hina Sakaji (now Shigenaka) became a member of the church.

Shortly after the U.S.-Japan war began on December 7, 1941, all people of Japanese origin were ordered to be removed from the West Coast. The final pre-evacuation church service was held on April 24, 1942. On April 30th our members, and others, were actually relocated, ultimately to the Gila Relocation Camp in Arizona. Our church building was left in the care of the Nazarene Church. After over four years, on August 28, 1946, Rev. Oshita was able to return to Santa Maria and on September 9, 1946, he opened the church as a hostel for returning Japanese people. Normal church activities shortly resumed and the ministry flourished.

On October 3, 1949, a special service was held to celebrate the 20-year anniversary of the church and the 20th year of Rev. Oshita's service. On the same date, the church was designated Self Supporting. By this time, the English-speaking Nisei young adults were taking more responsibility in church affairs. In 1954, Santa Maria born Rev. Paul Hagiya, who had earlier interned as a youth pastor in our church, was appointed our first Nisei pastor. He co-pastored with Rev. Oshita until Oshita's retirement in 1957, and continued as solo pastor until 1959. It was during Rev. Hagiya's tenure that the church's worship services and other functions changed from mostly Japanese language to mostly English.

The church continued growing during the Oshita-Hagiya years. On May 15, 1955, the church was incorporated into the Pacific Japanese Provisional Annual Conference of the Methodist Church. It was renamed Christ Methodist Church. In 1964, the churches of the Japanese Provisional Conference were absorbed into their respective regional conferences of the Methodist Church at large. Thus, we became a part of the Santa Barbara District of the Southern California-Arizona Annual Conference (now called the California-Pacific Annual Conference of the United Methodist Church).

In terms of membership participation, the peak years of the church were in the 1950s to mid-1960s during which church membership reached a range of 130 to 140, and Sunday School enrollment exceeded 100. In the late 1960s and 1970s, church membership and activities decreased somewhat as the younger Japanese families assimilated into surrounding communities, and a number of people moved to the larger urban areas. In the 1980s and 1990s, significant regrowth was achieved and has been mostly sustained into the present time.

As a church, although we treasure our Japanese heritage, we recognize that in these times we should be an all-inclusive church. In our church publications we call ourselves "A Church for All People".

In 2011, Rev. Dr. Anna Crews Camphouse was moved by the recent disasters in Japan to find a way to send help. Camphouse's calling, as minister of Christ United Methodist Church, led to the formation of the Japan Earthquake Tsunami Support (JETS) organization. Dr. Robert Yoshioka is the JETS co-chair.

> May God grant us the wisdom to follow his leading,
> and grant us a renewed spirit as we advance
> His kingdom through our church.

CHRIST UNITED METHODIST CHURCH
219 Mary Drive
Santa Maria, California

CHAPTER ELEVEN

THE CHURCH OF JESUS CHRIST
OF LATTER-DAY SAINTS

SANTA MARIA, CALIFORNIA, STAKE

INTRODUCTION

Although called "LDS" or "Mormon", the full and complete name of the church is "The Church of Jesus Christ of Latter-day Saints".   To understand the structure of the Mormon Church, a few definitions are needed:

1.   A "Stake" is the equivalent of a "Diocese", with a Stake President who reports to the Church Headquarters in Salt Lake City, Utah.   In Santa Maria, William Ridgeway is Stake President.

2.   A "Ward" is the equivalent of a "Parish", with a Bishop who oversees a ward. There are currently four wards in Santa Maria (one of which is for young singles).   The four current Bishops are: Clark Cashmore, Heber Perrett, Jeff Sais, and Kirk Leishman.

3.   A "Branch" is a small congregation of the church.   A Branch President presides over each Branch.   Marcelo Predazzi is the Branch President in the Spanish congregation at this time.

4.   A "Chapel" is a building that typically serves two or more wards or branches. There are currently two chapels in Santa Maria: one at 908 E. Sierra Madre and one at 1219 Oak Knoll Road.

5.   The "Relief Society" is a Women's Auxiliary.   It is currently led by Bebi Moncur.   It is one of the largest women's service organizations in the world.   They assist the sick, the poor, the widowed, etc. and are active in spiritual matters.

One interesting aspect of the Mormon Church: ALL MEMBERS SERVE WITHOUT PAY OR REMUNERATION.   All are volunteers and most have full-time jobs, contributing much to the communities they are in.

The Book of Mormon, subtitled Another Testament of Jesus Christ, is used alongside the Bible in services and education.   Mormons use the King James version of the Bible.

In 1920, there were only 134 members of the Mormon church scattered throughout the tri-county (Ventura, Santa Barbara, San Luis Obispo) area.   In 1928 the first local branch organized in San Luis Obispo, and the Santa Maria members attended there until 1934.

In 1934, Dr. Edmund Crowley was called as Branch President of the new Santa Maria Branch of the church.   They met in a rented hall on Main Street near the flagpole.

Dr. and Edna Crowley later donated the lot on the Southeast corner of Miller and Cook Streets for the first LDS chapel in town.

After World War II, Ralph Adams, a well-known magician, was one of the branch presidents and he led the fundraising for the Miller Street Chapel.

FIRST SANTA MARIA CHAPEL.
*Soon after World War II, fundraising began for the Church
building construction at the corner of Cook and Miller Streets.*

At times during the above period, the Minerva Club was rented for dances.   The LDS still have dances to this day.   Their youth and friends attend and dance the night away.

In 1963, the Santa Maria Stake was organized by Elder Harold B. Lee of the Quorum of Twelve Apostles.   He later became President of the church.   At that time, there were two wards in Santa Maria and two in Lompoc, with a branch in Solvang.   Clayton Call was the first Stake President in Santa Maria.

In 1964, a Spanish-speaking Branch of the church was organized in Santa Maria.   They meet in Ward I (908 E. Sierra Madre).

When the new Oak Knolls Chapel was dedicated February 16, 1968, the chapel at Miller and Cook was sold to the Salvation Army.

The Young Adult Ward was organized in 1983.   This is a congregation for those aged 18-30 who are single.

THE FIRST MORMON CHAPEL IN SANTA MARIA

Lots of people recognize our first chapel at the corner of Cook and Miller Streets as the Salvation Army church.   But a number of people still remember it as the first "Mormon Church" in Santa Maria.

The long and arduous path traveled in getting this first chapel constructed is well documented in the LDS history files. Thankfully, Mormons are excellent at keeping records.

They catered dinners for various businesses, held dances, entered floats in the County Fair Parade (this was before the Elks took over the parade), joined with other ministers in radio talk shows, etc. to accumulate money to do the construction. Most of the labor was provided by volunteers.

The chapel was finished in 1949 and dedicated in 1950, debt free. They started with $2,000 in the bank and finished the building, completely furnished, with a little less than $2,000 in the bank!

SOME RECENT HISTORY AND ACTIVITIES OF THE CHURCH

The Mormon Church officially launched its Helping Hands program in 1998, setting aside special days on which volunteers would fan out and do good deeds throughout the world. It originally targeted emergency situations in which a local response was essential. But it doesn't limit itself to emergencies. It strives to engage volunteers of all religious faiths in the common goal of making their communities better and stronger.

COMMUNITY CELEBRATION OF THE NATIVITY.
This annual event has been hosted by the LDS Church for the last 20 years.

On April 30, 2011, about 250 members of the Mormon Church filled Los Flores Ranch Park (south of Orcutt), attired in bright yellow work vests and a spirit of charity, to complete projects around the park.

The Mormon Church is one of the largest supporters of Boy Scouting in the Santa Maria Valley and annually hosts a Merit Badge Pow Wow that attracts over 200 scouts from all over the central coast, most of whom are not LDS.

LDS headquarters in Salt Lake City has long been renowned for their work and vast resources in genealogy research. What is less well-known, is that the Sierra Madre Chapel right here in Santa Maria has resources in genealogy open to the public as well.

MUSIC has always played a huge role in the Mormon Church. Is there anyone who hasn't heard the beautiful music of the Mormon Tabernacle Choir? Music is an important part of our local Mormon churches. Since their beginnings, they have been active in choirs, musicals, etc., and remain so today.

And speaking of music, for the last 20 years the LDS Church has hosted The Community Celebration of the Nativity in Santa Maria. Besides an hour-long musical program with choirs from other churches, schools, and community groups, there has been a display of well over 100 crèches (Nativity Sets) from families in the community, and outside a live Nativity with actors and a few animals. It runs for two nights with different groups each night. A capacity crowd comes every year!

A NATIVITY SET AT THE ANNUAL CELEBRATION.
This Nativity Set is one of many on display at the
Community Celebration of the Nativity in Santa Maria.

Since WWII, the LDS members in Santa Maria have hosted a breakfast on the 4th of July. It was initially for the servicemen to have something to do that day. It has evolved into a grand reunion. Around 300 folks show up!

Much of the material for this chapter was gleaned from Louise Newbold's book, *Santa Maria California Stake, The Church of Jesus Christ of Latter-day Saints: Silver Anniversary History*, published in 1991. The remainder was provided by Mike Spears and Marilyn Rosenlof. The pictures of the annual Christmas Nativity (one live outdoor and one still indoor display) were loaned by Mike Spears.

CHAPTER TWELVE

PACIFIC CHRISTIAN CENTER
(FORMERLY FIRST ASSEMBLY OF GOD)

INTRODUCTION

The church was originally the First Assembly of God with Charles Dobbins as its first pastor in 1936. The pastors following Charles Dobbins were: Tom Ming, L.E. Halverson, Malcum Edmundson, C.J. Brown, James W. Dollins, E. J. Krumpe, Harris Lidstrand, Norman Field, Jerry Clark, Lloyd Huf, Timothy Lake, Robert E. Palmer, Ben Ellsworth, and the current pastor, Robert Bloom.

Records are scant on the early days of the church. One very old picture (exact location unknown) appears to be a huge tent.

The church relocated four times as it grew. Today it is located at 3435 Santa Maria Way with easy access to the freeway. It sits on twelve and one-half acres.

The name change came about in the 1980s to reflect the growing vision and purpose of the church. Today it is a huge center of activities.

On October 9, 2011 Pacific Christian Center celebrated its 75th Anniversary.

PASTORAL STAFF

Pastor Rev. Rick Bloom:

Under the leadership of Pastor Bloom, Pacific Christian Center has made an amazing turnaround. From a church that was burdened with debt and bordering on "going under" it has emerged as a large and powerful church in Santa Maria. And their sizeable mortgage has been paid off.

The army of volunteers that conduct ministries are the real heroes in the success of this huge church. It would be impossible to mention them all, but the Assistant Pastors that Rev. Rick Bloom leads are as follows:

Associate Pastor Joe Hunt:

"Pastor Joe" reports that it has been an amazing year for the Pacific Christian School. The economy has been a challenge but the school's enrollment has been holding steady. Each day 350-400 children step onto the campus and receive an education based on a Biblical worldview, challenging them to grow as Jesus grew, "in wisdom and stature, and in favor with God and men."

Joe reports there was incredible support with fundraising efforts and scholarship donations. Their Dinner Auction grossed over $60,000 once again.

Proceeds from these fundraisers help with projects all over the campus. The software and set-up of 68 computers donated by Brandman University is one example. And donations to the Jacob Knight Scholarship helped more than 50 students last year.

The staff at the Pacific Christian School is truly amazing. These dedicated teachers and support personnel work long hours with servant-hearted attitudes – and within the constraints of a very tight budget. Vice Principal Monica Thorpe deserves high honors for outstanding effort.

On the church side, Joe is equally proud of the Worship Team members, including all the support personnel. Each week, a dozen or so musicians and technicians come early to offer their musical gifts, or minister in a host of other ways – sound, lights, video…

The sound and media committee is making progress toward improvement of the sanctuary systems. Don Swanson, Steve Campbell and Richard Jamison have spent many hours in research and planning, and have recently contracted for the engineering/design phase. This coming year should be very exciting.

Assistant Pastor Phil Young – Children and Outreach:

Children's Ministries of Pacific Christian Center is referred to as "pcKidz" and is under the supervision of the Children's Pastor. PcKidz covers children from birth through 5th Grade.

WEEKLY MINISTRIES

Sundays:

On Sundays, nursery childcare is available for all morning and evening services for children infant through three years of age. The Pacific Christian Center Nursery is staffed with qualified and approved workers and volunteers. At the age of 4 the children are eligible to move to the Sunday morning Lil'Kidz program. This is a curriculum based program with music, crafts and teaching Bible truths at the child's level of understanding.

Kidz Church covers children 6 years of age through 5th Grade. This is a high-energy Rally service with media and teacher based curriculum – filled with music, games, Bible truths and activities.

pcKidz Choir rehearses and presents an outstanding music program annually. This choir is directed by the Music Pastor, Maureen Rickman.

Wednesdays:

Wednesday night is Family Night – with ministry for the whole family. The boys and girls look forward to Wednesday night all week! M-Pact is an award-driven girls program, and Royal Rangers is an award-driven, Christian based scouting program for the boys.

Other:

In addition to these weekly ministries, quarterly and annual events are offered. LIVEWIRE is a family rally which takes place two or three times a year. This is a time for kids and parents to come together and enjoy games, activity, food, and a Gospel Rally.

ADDITIONAL PROGRAMS AND ACTIVITIES

Summer Fund for the Kids. Vacation Bible School is usually scheduled during the last week of July. We have been offering MEGA SPORTS CAMP. This program gives opportunity for skill development in sports and daily Bible teaching.

Harvest Fest takes place the end of October. This is an evening filled with fun activities – games, prizes, costumes, hayrides, and lots of good food. All of the various ministries of PCC help make this an exciting night for the entire church.

Metro Kids is offered weekly at two locations in Inner-City Santa Maria. Working teams go into the neighborhoods with a Gospel Rally, songs, prizes, games and fun. Eighty to 100 kids show up at each location.

Angel Food is a weekly program that provides food to families in need in the Santa Maria area. PCC workers and volunteers work with our local Spanish churches in preparation and distribution of food to families in need. At the distribution site, there is also a church service in Spanish for anyone who would like to attend.

MUSIC MINISTER MAUREEN RICKMAN

The Music Department, under the direction of Pastor "Moe" has experienced a year of growth and ministry.

The adult Celebration Choir continues to lead PCC into God's presence on Sundays, as well as on Easter, at Christmas and Patriotic musicals. Maureen also directs the Children's Choir.

STUDENT MINISTER JEFF SEELEY

Under the leadership of Pastor Jeff Seeley, several distinct areas of ministry have developed:

JV (6th-8th grades). JV is a ministry JUST FOR 6th-8th grade students.   It is all about connecting with friends and with God.

VARSITY (9th-12th grades). Varsity is all about mentoring and coaching students in their relationship with God and in life.

OVERTIME (Young Adults).   This is a place where they build lasting connections, deepen their relationship with God, and live out their faith.

PACIFIC CHRISTIAN PRESCHOOL. Maureen Calderwood is the Director of the Preschool. She asks for prayers for the preschool teachers as they share the gospel with our precious little ones and their families.

RAINBOW MINISTRY. Under the direction of Alex & Sarah Cruz.   This year the Rainbow Ministry celebrates 8 years serving the guests at Good Samaritan Shelter.   Alex and Sarah want to thank the many volunteers from PCC that cook, serve, and minister to the families in need.   Rainbow Ministry served over 2,500 meals at the Shelter this year.

PRIMETIMER'S MINISTRY. Under the direction of Harvey and Reba Morris.   This group plans and implements a variety of activities for the mature adults.   Their motto: "Serving Christ While Serving Others."

CELEBRATE RECOVERY. Under the leadership of Frank and Julie Claybough.   This program is to fellowship and celebrate God's healing power in our lives through eight recovery principles and the Christ-centered 12 steps.

VISITATION AND PASTORAL CARE - PASTOR BRIAN LOWE: Brian spends a lot of time in hospitals.   And nursing homes.   Not as an occupant.   His is the friendly, caring face you will probably encounter if YOU are an occupant!   You will probably see his smiling face if you are a new member of PCC.   Or maybe you were just a visitor.   Thank God for people like Brian!   Hospitals and nursing homes can be very, very lonely places.

"TO KNOW CHRIST AND TO MAKE HIM KNOWN"

PACIFIC CHRISTIAN CENTER
3435 Santa Maria Way
Santa Maria, California 93455

Services: Sunday AM 9 & 10:30
Sunday PM 6:00
"Family Night" is 6:45 Wednesdays

CHAPTER THIRTEEN

CORNERSTONE - A CHURCH OF THE NAZARENE

Though the Church of the Nazarene first began in Pilot Point, Texas, in October of 1908, its local Santa Maria congregants, which included only four charter members, came together in 1937 at an in-home Bible study on Donovan Road, hosted by a Nazarene couple from the Central Valley.

The church officially organized in 1938, and Nicholas Hull became its first pastor. Because the congregation was outgrowing home gatherings, worship moved to a single rented room at the Moose Lodge on West El Camino. As the church body grew to about thirty, they expanded out to the main dance floor and the bar area, and they needed to arrive every Sunday morning at 6 a.m. to clean up the bar mess from the night before. One longtime church attendee related the story that the Lodge also housed a slot machine and one of the young Sunday School boys deposited his offering there and received a payout in return. The congregation worshipped in this location for three years.

In 1942, shortly after the start of World War II, the Japanese Methodist Church on North Mary Drive, behind Stewart Oldsmobile, became available because the Japanese people in Santa Maria had been sent to internment camps. Vandenberg Air Force Base at that time was called Camp Cook. The church made the Mary Drive location their home for five years and continued to grow.

Realizing their need to think about building their own facility, property was purchased at the corner of East Mill and North Vine. In 1945, construction began on the church sanctuary at that site. Building materials were hard to get because of the war, so two ladies from the church went from business to business getting donations to buy church pews and chairs for the people to sit on. In February of 1949, the worshippers held their first services at the Mill and Vine address. The Education and Fellowship wings were added to the property in 1951-52.

In early 1953, the church, in need of carpeting for their basement, purchased carpet for $1.50 a square yard from Dudley-Hoffman Mortuary, with arrangements to pay it off by the month. To this day, the local Nazarene Church continues to experience a favorable relationship with the mortuary and its staff.

Over the following years, there were thoughts that the church either needed to expand in its present location or it needed to consider relocating elsewhere. In 1962 the church had opened a preschool at their Mill and Vine address, and this preschool was to enjoy a good reputation in the community for many years to come.

The purchase of five-plus acres of property at Bradley Road and East Sierra Madre became a reality in 1975. Hancock College did all of the site preparation and grading at no cost to the church, so the students involved could have the experience.   Reverend David Kennedy coordinated the construction endeavor, and in 1977 the first building on the property was begun.   Originally intended as a parsonage, it actually became the new location of the church's preschool.   About nine months after the completion of the preschool, the church needed to vacate their Mill and Vine property and find another place to worship.   God opened the doors for the congregation to use the Hancock College cafeteria on Sunday mornings, at minimal cost for the utilities and the janitorial fees, plus Hancock did all the set up and teardown for free.   The piano was rolled in every Sunday as the choir came in, after they had completed their practice time out in the hallway.   The church's own preschool building was used on Sunday evenings, with members setting up chairs and altars every Sunday afternoon.   Altars were transported back and forth from the preschool to Hancock College for nine months.

One of the defining moments for the Santa Maria Church of the Nazarene was in March of 1979 when Reverend David Kennedy, who was in the midst of coordinating the new church relocation and building project, lost his wife, Estela Carmen Kennedy, in a Swift Aire Lines plane crash in the ocean off Marina del Rey.   Estela had been loved in the community and by her church family, so of course there was widespread grief, but the loss also served to cement the resolve of her husband, and her church, to pursue construction of the sanctuary building (completed in 1979) and the gymnasium/education wing (completed in 1988) which is still serving the Nazarene congregation today.   She was remembered with the dedication of an upstairs prayer room which displays her picture.

Santa Maria Church of the Nazarene has continued their active ministries to children, youth, men, women and senior adults.   As a revitalized vision of ministry to the community of Santa Maria began to take shape in 2009, the church name was changed to Cornerstone, A Church of the Nazarene.   The new sense of purpose deserved a new name, but still needed to retain the basic identity of a Nazarene Church for those in the community surrounding it.   Cornerstone today feels that they are aptly defined by their statement of mission:

LOVE GOD, LOVE OTHERS, SERVE THE COMMUNITY

CORNERSTONE – A CHURCH OF THE NAZARENE
1026 E. Sierra Madre Ave.
Santa Maria, California   93454
Phone: 922-1919

CORNERSTONE – A CHURCH OF THE NAZARENE.
Construction was completed on the new sanctuary building in 1979.

CHAPTER FOURTEEN

JEHOVAH'S WITNESSES

The history of Jehovah's Witnesses in the Santa Maria Valley began in the late 1930's. One family, in which the father and two sons were active preachers, was assigned by the Watchtower Bible and Tract Society to begin a ministry in this area. Their sphere of activity encompassed a large area, Solvang and Lompoc, and Northward to parts of San Luis Obispo County. They carried out this work by following the method Christ Jesus, our Lord, taught his disciples and the Christians in the first century, preaching the Good News of the Kingdom publicly and from house to house.

As time moved on, it became obvious that, with the interest growing among the good-hearted people in the Santa Maria area, a meeting location was needed. This was in harmony with the Apostolic command found in the book of Hebrews, chapter 10, verses 23 through 25, to assemble together with fellow believers. Thus began a number of years with the meetings being held at an upstairs location above the B & B Coffee Shop, located next to the former Santa Maria Theater, on the west side of Broadway. Later, as more and more people began to search for real Bible truth to improve their lives, the meeting location was moved to a garage on Elizabeth Street.

Now, as the year 1955 arrived, it became clear the congregation had outgrown the meeting place once again. Therefore, the providential decision was made to build a brand new Kingdom Hall, as the buildings used by the Jehovah's Witnesses had begun to be called. This new location was at 610 West Church Street, which building is still being used today by the Tagalog Congregation, and other language groups.

Although the area of preaching kept growing smaller, due to the fact that the congregations to the North and South of Santa Maria took over those sections closer to their own towns, the friendly Santa Maria people continued to respond to the active preaching work by the nearly 300 Jehovah's Witnesses. Once more it became obvious that another meeting place was needed. So, in December of 1971, the work of constructing the Kingdom Hall at 555 East Foster Road began. The dedication to Jehovah God of this very fine building took place in July of 1972.

KINGDOM HALL 1956.
Located at 610 West Church St., this facility is still used today by the Tagalog Congregation, and other language groups.

Again, the years continued to roll by, and many Spanish and English-speaking congregations were formed continually. As a matter of fact, to accommodate the truth-loving people in Santa Maria, there were 2, 3, and 4 congregations meeting in the same Kingdom Hall, at staggered times.

We believe God's guidance became obvious again, as a large piece of land, south of the Santa Maria River, near the San Luis Obispo County line, and the bridge, became available.

Thus, in 1990, a large, beautiful building was completed, located at 333 Hidden Pines Way. The hall accommodates four separate Kingdom Halls, under one roof. Several times a year the partitions inside the

JEHOVAH'S WITNESS NEW FACILITY 1972.
The dedication of this facility. located at 555 East Foster Road,, took place in July 1972.

building are opened to form a large auditorium, with seating for over 1,000 bible students, during special conventions. This building has been remodeled a couple of times, most recently in 2010, for the purpose of having schools to properly train the many brothers who are looking after individual congregations, which now are over 12, with about 2,500 people attending.

SANTA MARIA'S MOST RECENT KINGDOM HALL.
This beautiful facility, located at 333 Hidden Pines Way, was completed in 1990, and has been through two remodeling projects since completion.

There are no salaried positions in the Kingdom Halls. All of the leaders serve on a volunteer basis.

During the reading of Jehovah's Witnesses history in the Santa Maria Valley, some may wonder, "Is this the extent of their activity?" By no means. Jehovah's Witnesses obey the command given in the book of Matthew, chapter 24, verse 14, to preach the good news of the kingdom worldwide. In addition to this, they are also conscious of Jesus command to make more disciples by teaching them and baptizing them, as His own words so forcefully expressed it in Matthew, chapter 28, verses 19 and 20. To accomplish such a great work, the preaching activity had to be expanded worldwide.

Beginning in the late 19th century people were sent out as missionaries to begin this worldwide activity. In 1943, great impetus was added to this work in the foreign countries when the Watchtower Bible School of Gilead was opened to train Jehovah's Witnesses as missionaries. This Gilead School consists of 6 months of intensive training for a foreign assignment. Part of this curriculum includes a reading of the entire Bible. Some language training is arranged for, but learning the language of the foreign country becomes more like "on-the-job training."

To date, about 7000 Jehovah's Witnesses have graduated from the Bible School of Gilead and have been sent out as missionaries worldwide. Currently, about half of those are still serving in their assignments. The reason so many have stayed so long in a foreign country is the fact that these missionaries view this as a lifetime career, not just a temporary assignment. The foreign country becomes their new permanent home.

There have been some people from Santa Maria who have entered this missionary work. Others here have close relatives who have been sent out to various places in the world for their assignments. Some time ago, a family sold home and possessions and moved to Bolivia to help people learn more about God's Word, the Bible, and become a part of the ever-growing fellowship of true worshipers.

Due to the very demanding life of a Christian missionary, many here locally cannot go to a foreign country because of family and other responsibilities. Therefore, many here have started learning another language, such as Tagalog, Hindu, and Arabic, in order to preach the Good News of the Kingdom to these smaller groups of people now living among us in Santa Maria.

Additionally, there is now an American Sign Language Congregation here in Santa Maria to aid the deaf in our area. Also, Jehovah's Witnesses have available much literature in the above-mentioned languages, including Braille and audio productions to aid the blind in Santa Maria.

We hope the above has whetted the appetite of the reader to attend some of the meetings in any of the Kingdom Halls in our friendly town of Santa Maria.

CHAPTER FIFTEEN

FIRST BAPTIST CHURCH

HISTORY

The church was started in early 1941, with five families meeting in homes for prayer until they started meeting in the Minerva Club building at the corner of Lincoln and Boone, under the name of Gospel Center. The church was organized in February of 1941. The first pastor was Rev. William Painter.

Under the leadership of Dr. J. Franklin Prewitt, the name was changed to the First Baptist Church of Santa Maria.

Some of the original members were Mr. and Mrs. Harry Nelson, Mrs. Sue Thompson, Marie and Lee Lauenstein, Barbara and Lee Fults, Miriam Houser, Ada Clark, Edna Weatherall, and Rev. and Mrs. Gettman.

The church property on the corner of Fesler and Vine was purchased for $1,800 in 1942, while Dr. Prewitt was pastor. Pastor Burton Reed assisted in building the first auditorium of the church, which faces Vine Street.

THE FIRST BAPTIST CHURCH.
This is the original building of the First Baptist Church, located at the corner of Fesler and Vine.

Rev. Glen Discoe was pastor for a short period after Pastor Reed. Rev. Ezra Hill was pastor for several years. Rev. Merle Booth was pastor when both units of the Sunday school were built, and also the main auditorium.

Under the leadership of Pastor Lepp, the Pine Grove Baptist Church property was purchased, and the first unit was built as a mission church.

In December of 1975, First Baptist sold their property on Fesler and Vine and moved the church out to 2970 Santa Maria Way, where they held services in a chapel in one of the seven VCA buildings.

GROUNDBREAKING CEREMONY.
Groundbreaking ceremony for new First Baptist Church Building. Photograph circa 1978.

The current church building was built in 1979 and remodeled in 2008. The current pastor is Dr. Jim Schettler, who moved here with his family in 2007 from Pensacola, FL.

BACKGROUND OF VALLEY CHRISTIAN ACADEMY

In the early 1960s, public schools began limiting the use of the Bible, even in Christmas and Easter celebrations. As a result, private schools, particularly church-related, were multiplying.

When Walter Lepp became pastor of First Baptist Church, he had a vision of a Christian day school. The church agreed and appointed a committee to study the feasibility of starting a school. They chose Valley Christian Academy as the school's name. One of those committee members, Cathy Reed, is still an active church member. A number of conservatives in the community became interested, resulting in community backing.

Valley Christian Academy (VCA) was started in September 1967 by holding classes in Pine Grove Church. At that time, Pine Grove was a mission church of First Baptist. The VCA opened with three teachers and 52 students, kindergarten through fourth grade.

The current church property (25 acres) located at 2970 Santa Maria Way was purchased in 1968, and building on the site quickly began. VCA was expanded from preschool through Grade 12. By 1979, VCA had its highest enrollment of 484 students in grades kindergarten through 12th grade.

The VCA property has grown to meet the ever-increasing needs of the community. In addition to the 11 buildings which house classrooms, office, chapel, library, garage, preschool, and a mobile home, there is a 900-seat auditorium, and a gymnasium.

A Talent Development class was initiated in 1982 to meet the needs of students with learning disabilities.

Spiritual Emphasis Week, along with Senior Missions Trips, and Ezra Leadership Camps, have helped maintain and enhance the spiritual focus of VCA.

PRESCHOOL

In 1968, Valley Christian Preschool was started using two classrooms from the VCA. Two years later, the Preschool moved into its own new building under the contracting of Bob Roinestad.

Longevity of the staff demonstrates their commitment to children. Three preschool teachers served extended tenures: Barbara Adkins for 25 years; Nancy Roinestad for over 30 years; and director Karen Payne for 17 years. The remodeling of the building and play yard through the years aided in the Preschool's continued demonstration of striving for excellence.

First Baptist Church's growth has been a journey of faith over the past 70 years, and it has played a key role in the betterment of Santa Maria.

FIRST BAPTIST CHURCH
2970 Santa Maria Way
Santa Maria, California 93455
(805) 937-8405

CHAPTER SIXTEEN

GRACE LUTHERAN CHURCH

HISTORY

Grace Lutheran had its beginnings in Santa Maria in 1938. Rev. August Hansen, Mission Director of the California and Nevada District, canvassed Santa Maria and found 17 Lutherans. Pastor Walter Loretz of San Luis Obispo led the work in Santa Maria.

The first worship occurred on February 20, 1938 at the Minerva Clubhouse. About three months later, worship moved to the Seventh-day Adventist building on West Fesler. On December 18, 1938, Grace Lutheran was formed.

On October 27, 1941, Grace Evangelical Lutheran Church was organized and incorporated. Charter membership consisted of 54 communicants and 17 VOTING members. (Women were not allowed a vote in those days).

In January of 1942, the place of worship was moved to the Camp Fire Girls Building at West Morrison and South Lincoln Streets. Services continued there for three years. A number of Servicemen attended. One old photo provided by Sandra Bunch and Gloria Byrd (identical twins whose parents and grandparents were charter members) shows a service being conducted in that building. Folding metal chairs seated the congregation. A ping-pong table, complete with net, paddles, and balls is in full view on the

CAMP FIRE GIRLS COTTAGE.
Grace Lutheran Church held services in this building for three years, 1942-1945. Photograph circa 1942.

left side of the congregation. A young boy is sitting sidewise in his metal chair staring longingly at the ping-pong table while the pastor is conducting the service!

Dedication of the Parish Hall at 420 East Fesler took place on August 26, 1945.

Members dedicated the present sanctuary of Grace Lutheran Church at 423 East Fesler on July 1, 1962.

In November 2008, the members of Grace Lutheran determined to remodel the old Parish Hall at 420 East Fesler (across the street) to bring it into conformance with current standards for accessibility and safety, as well as modernization of plumbing and fixtures. It now serves as the church nursery/ preschool.

MINISTRIES OF GRACE LUTHERAN CHURCH, SANTA MARIA

Support to Grace Lutheran Nursery School:

Members man a fireworks booth in Santa Maria to raise support for the Nursery School. They also sponsor other fundraisers such as fish dinners, enchilada sales and pie auctions. Proceeds from these fundraisers assist several families with "scholarships", so their children can attend the preschool.

"Church" at Good Samaritan Shelter:

For several years, we have had a weekly activity for children ages 3-12 at the transition shelter of the Good Samaritan Shelter. This includes a Bible story, songs, crafts and healthy snack. This began in 2004 with a Vacation Bible School we ran for the children at the shelter for a week. They enjoyed the activity so much we decided to continue the support on a weekly basis.

Community Garden:

A member of Grace Lutheran has a 10-acre spread off Telephone Road. There he prepares and fertilizes a large garden plot 120 feet by 60 feet. Members of Grace Lutheran plant, tend and harvest vegetables from that plot and transport the produce to the kitchen of the Salvation Army or the Santa Barbara County Food Bank. Last year we donated over 1600 pounds of produce to the community.

Lutheran Border Concerns Ministry:

Every summer, youth and adults travel from several churches on the Central Coast to Tijuana, Mexico. Pastor Burch of Grace Lutheran leads these trips, as he has fluency in Spanish. There we construct several houses for poor people living on the growing fringe of Tijuana. We also do a two or three day Vacation Bible School, which includes Bible stories, crafts, songs and snacks.

Support to Casa Hogar Sion, Tijuana:

During one of our trips to Mexico, we became acquainted with an orphanage in Eastern Tijuana. The orphanage receives no Government support, but depends on donations from the private sector. We have taken donations to buy new clothing, have done food drives and provided Christmas gifts for various groups of children in the orphanage. This last Christmas, we transported close to a ton of beans, rice, canned fruits and vegetables to the orphanage.

Disaster Relief:

Following Hurricane Katrina in New Orleans, we organized three teams of students from Cal Poly, Cuesta College and Concordia Irvine under the leadership of skilled carpenters, electricians and plumbers. They traveled to and stayed at Camp Restore on the campus of Prince of Peace Lutheran Church in East New Orleans during their winter break. There they "mucked out" houses, rewired, dry walled, painted, cleaned yards, and any number of other tasks needed to restore homes to livability.

Remembering Our Warriors:

One of our Lutheran chaplains in Afghanistan wrote how deployed men and women miss certain "comforts" from home...snacks, batteries, wet wipes, etc. Church members brought donations to send off to the chaplain to distribute to his task force. We recently mailed five large USPS boxes filled with goodies. We continue to accept donations as we will support two young men in the EOD unit who are deploying from Vandenberg AFB.

Food Distribution Program:

Several members participate in the community food distribution program. They meet at another church in Santa Maria, bag the groceries and deliver the food to designated recipients.

Sunday worship services are conducted in English at 9:30 A.M. The worship service in Spanish immediately follows at 11:00 A.M. Both services are conducted by Pastor Burch.

GRACE LUTHERAN CHURCH
423 East Fesler St.
Santa Maria, California 93454

CHAPTER SEVENTEEN

GRACE BAPTIST CHURCH

In July 1950, a small group from First Baptist Church began meeting in homes until they organized as Grace Baptist Church. With a membership of 44, under the leadership of Rev. Glenn Discoe, services were held in the Seventh-day Adventist Church building on West Fesler.

In 1951, services were moved to the Moose Lodge. During this early period, members were required to arrive for services very early on Sunday morning, air out and clean the facility from Saturday night's patrons.

On Labor Day 1957, the church began construction of a sanctuary on a large vacant lot they had purchased on Alvin Avenue. Because many of the congregation gave sacrificially of their time, talents and money, the sanctuary was completed 22 months later, completely debt free.

In July 1965, the church purchased the house at 205 West Alvin. This house was originally the manse for the Presbyterian Church, and had been moved to this location in the mid-1950s.

On July 13, 1975, the church celebrated its 25th anniversary with a special service and banquet. Many of the people who had moved away from the area came back to help celebrate.

In April 1987, the first Spanish-speaking assembly was officially started under the leadership of Juan Cortez as pastor.

On August 5, 1990, the church celebrated its 40th anniversary with a special service and afternoon barbeque.

An AWANA group was formed and was quite successful. It continues to this day. This is a children's group, age three through 6th grade.

The church held many musical events. On February 24, 1980, a choir group called Somethin' Special, for fourth through eighth grade youth was added to the musical ministries. This group was discontinued at some point in history.

In November 1973, the church called Ron Inscho as director of youth/music/Christian education. And January 6, 1974, a choir group called New Horizons, for senior high and college age youth, was added to the church's music ministries.

GRACE BAPTIST OFFERS A LARGE SELECTION.
Grace Baptist Church offers many youth and musical programs and ministries.

It was under Ron Inscho's direction that a beautiful and highly unusual musical event was born - THE LIVING CHRISTMAS TREE.

This annual event was quite spectacular and tickets had to be obtained in advance for specific performances. The Christmas tree was set up in the choir loft, each singer wore a "bib" so that only their face was showing between the branches of the tree. The younger singers were placed in the higher "perches" among the branches.

Down in the orchestra "pit" someone had to stand with cue cards for the singers to follow. The orchestra members were made up of musicians from all over town, but the singers up in the trees were all Grace Baptists.

Patti Lynn (Allan Hancock College) worked with Ron Inscho on getting the orchestra players (a few that come to mind were: Jim Tobin, piano; Jed Beebe, violin; Michelle Winger, violin; Bruce Kurley, trumpet; Walt Stier, French horn; Patti Lynn, oboe).

The need for a much larger church facility became evident in 1998. The congregation voted to look for a much larger site for a new church building. On November 19, 1999, the church closed escrow on property on South College Drive and East McCoy.

April 13, 2003, a Ground Breaking Ceremony was held on College & McCoy. Charter members Janie Sanford and Fern McIntosh, Dan Lockhart (representing the Dr. Jack

Lockhart family) and Pastor Duane Johnson officially broke ground for the new building.

On January 9, 2005, Grace Baptist held their Grand Opening Celebration with 599 people in attendance.

The official dedication service took place February 20, 2005.

GRACE BAPTIST CHURCH

Many new families joined the church and on Easter Sunday, April 12, 2009, a third Sunday morning service was added.

The church has continued to grow and the approximately 32,000 square foot structure is once again overflowing. A new approximately 9,900 square foot Christian Education Building is nearing completion and the church hopes to dedicate the facility on July 3, 2011. This building provides for a youth center, adult Sunday school rooms, and a 200-seat worship center.

The music director for the traditional service is David Rackley. The music director for the contemporary service is Chet Harter.

Grace Baptist has continued to grow throughout the years, providing guidance and Christian fellowship throughout its history. It also plays host to many concerts and other cultural activities in the community.

When future history books of Santa Maria's churches are written, Grace Baptist will take its place as one which planned ahead for the explosive population growth in the Santa Maria Valley.

THE LIVING CHRISTMAS TREE, DECEMBER 2001.
The singing at this annual event was performed by the Grace Baptist Choir, with the assistance of orchestra members from throughout the Santa Maria area.

GRACE BAPTIST CHURCH
605 East McCoy Lane
Santa Maria, California 93455
(805) 925-2671

CHAPTER EIGHTEEN

BETHEL LUTHERAN CHURCH

In 1960, the AMERICAN LUTHERAN CHURCH decided to establish a mission congregation in the growing community of Santa Maria. Rev. Ernest Zoerb was called to serve as the mission pastor.

Among the people visited by Rev. Zoerb were Mr. and Mrs. Raymond Duncan. They became charter members of the congregation, and when Ray, the survivor, passed away in 1983, Bethel became the benefactor of their entire estate. The current church library has been dedicated to Ray and Mabel Duncan.

The first worship service of the congregation was held on October 23, 1960 at the home of Mr. and Mrs. Clinton Cromwell, with Pastor Zoerb preaching from the Old Testament on the history of the word "Bethel", which means "House of God". There were 26 people present at that service.

On March 12, 1961, ground was broken on a 5-acre site at 624 East Camino Colegio. On March 20, 1961, the congregation was officially formed. The first building occupied was an educational and multipurpose building originally called Zoerb Hall, which is now the kitchen. Formal dedication of the buildings, including the sanctuary, occurred on November 5, 1961.

During the early years, the women of Bethel organized a Quilting Ministry. This ministry has continued to the present time, distributing hundreds of quilts through Lutheran World Relief and other organizations that serve people in need.

Through the years, Pastor Zoerb's knowledge and love of botany led to the planting of almost 300 trees, including 38 species, on the acreage surrounding Bethel.

BETHEL LUTHERAN CHURCH.
Formally dedicated in 1961, the facility still serves Bethel's congregation.

Rev. Paul E. Johnson was installed as pastor on July 2, 1970. During the time he was pastor, the congregation began to make plans for construction of the education building.

Rev. Sig Sandrock was installed as pastor on August 19, 1973. In November of 1973, the Bethel Prayer Chain was started and still exists today. During Rev. Sandrock's tenure the education building was completed, the Bethel Library was started with donations from members, and the first Congregational Bethel Retreat was held at El Camino Pines.

Rev. Robert A. Rod was installed as pastor on January 1, 1977. During his tenure, a long-range planning and building committee was established, the chancel was furnished with a new altar, lectern, pulpit, and baptismal font crafted by Bethel member Morris Schaffert, and the stained glass windows in the front and back of the sanctuary were installed.

On September 1, 1980, Rev. Jerome C. Trelstad was installed as pastor. During his tenure, a master development plan of the property was approved, and the sanctuary was refurbished. And in 1983, the current church offices, fireside room, and library were constructed.

The congregation also entered into sponsorship of Ed and Karen Scott in Bangladesh, who served under the World Mission Prayer League. The relationship with the Scott family continues to the present time, as they serve Lutheran Health Care Bangladesh near the communities of Dhaka and Dumki.

After 38 years of dedicated service, Pastor Trelstad retired from parish ministry in August 1996. He has continued to serve the Lord as a volunteer builder of homes for Habitat for Humanity in several locations around the country, as a short-term missionary in Bangladesh, as a vacancy pastor in New Zealand, as leader in assembling people from several churches to serve as short-term missionaries at the Lutheran Bible School in Martin, Slovakia, including participation in the Mission, as leader in assembling people from several churches to serve on a Global Mission Outreach Team, etc. Pastor Trelstad and his wife remain members of Bethel.

Rev. Carl Nielsen was installed as pastor on July 1, 1997, and is our current pastor. Numerous new activities, expanded services, and refurbishments have taken place during his tenure.

Rev. Nielsen participated in a "pulpit exchange" on February 27, 2011, when six clergy traded churches for a Sunday morning. It gave all the congregations a sense of the "bigger church".

Bethel was established in 1961 with 82 charter members. We have a great history but we are not resting on it. We are looking ahead with excitement and anticipation to what God has planned for us in the future.

BETHEL LUTHERAN CHURCH
624 East Camino Colegio
Santa Maria, California 93454
(805) 922-6601

CHAPTER NINETEEN

ST. LOUIS DE MONTFORT
CATHOLIC CHURCH

HISTORY

The history of St. Louis de Montfort Catholic Church officially began on March 22, 1963. The Archbishop of Los Angeles, Cardinal Francis McIntyre, seeing the growth in the Orcutt-Santa Maria area, divided St. Mary's parish into two parts. St. Louis de Montfort was the name given to our new parish. The parish boundaries were established as south from Betteravia Road to Los Alamos; from Black Road and Highway 1 on the west, across the valley eastward to the Cuyama Hills in the east. Rev. Vincent McCabe, Associate Pastor of St. Mary's in Santa Maria, was named the first Pastor of St. Louis de Montfort.

A ten-acre site on the corner of Clark Avenue and Harp Road was purchased. Until the planned facilities could be built, Fr. McCabe conducted services in an old airport mess hall at Goodwin and Industrial Roads.

In January 1964, the 8-classroom grammar school constructed on the southern part of the parish site was opened. Services were then moved to the school buildings, using the present 6th, 7th and 8th grade classrooms. In September 1964, the school opened with grades 1-4, and each year a new grade was added. From 1964 to 2004, the school had been staffed by Daughters of Mary and Joseph. As of 2004 a lay principal, Mrs. Kathy Crow, was the administrator.

ST. LOUIS DE MONTFORT CATHOLIC CHURCH

To accommodate Fr. McCabe's living quarters and provide office space, a residential house on Bauer Avenue, parallel to Clark Avenue, was purchased.

As the school was soon going to be growing, a church was needed. So, groundbreaking ceremonies for the actual church were held in March 1964. The first Mass in the new church was celebrated January 30, 1966, by Fr. Vincent McCabe. Two years later, on February 4, 1968, the church and school were formally dedicated by Cardinal Francis McIntyre. The first Associate Pastor, Fr. Edmond Renehan, came in 1966 and remained until 1969. From 1965-1975 St. Louis de Montfort grew into a functioning, thriving and expanding parish. In 1975, Fr McCabe was transferred to San Roque Parish in Santa Barbara and Fr. Martin McGovern, another Archdiocesan priest, was sent to replace Fr. McCabe; however, he resigned due to ill health within nine months.

The Josephite Congregation then petitioned the Archbishop for permission to assume the administration of the parish. This was granted and Fr. Anthony Runtz, CJ, was named Pastor in 1975. The Josephite Fathers have been responsible for the administration of the parish ever since.

ST. LOUIS DE MONTFORT INTERIOR.
A view of the Sanctuary from the balcony.

Many changes and improvements took place under Fr. Anthony's tenure. In 1977, a parish hall was built and named after the longtime parish housekeeper, Mildred Jeffers. In 1980, a rectory was built and the school playground was finished. A Parish Council was formed and a variety of ministries and services to the parishioners began to function.

In 1980, St. Louis de Montfort was given the special privilege of celebrating the ordination of Fr. Michael Biewend, CJ. This was the first ordination of a priest in the Santa Maria-Orcutt area.

Since then, we have been honored with three more Josephite ordinations: Fr. Thomas Elewant, CJ - August 1986; Fr. Ed Jalbert, CJ - August 1987; and our first locally raised and educated Fr. Tim Lane, CJ, in May 1995. Fr. Tim was a graduate of our parish school and the Josephite-administered St. Joseph High School.

In 1985, Fr. Guillermo Garcia, CJ, was named Pastor. With Archbishop (now Cardinal) Mahoney's arrival in the Archdiocese, the idea of a convocation was encouraged, and St. Louis de Montfort Parish held its first Convocation Fair in 1987. This was the beginning of many on-going pastoral projects, and included the adoption of a parish mission statement and motto: "Building one Family in Christ."

Fr. Garcia left in October 1990, to assume the position of Superior General of the Josephite Congregation, and Fr. Mark Newman, CJ, was appointed Pastor. Fr. Mark had been principal of St. Joseph High School.

In October 2001, Fr. Charles Hofschulte, CJ, succeeded Fr. Mark and is currently the Pastor. Fr. Charles had succeeded Fr. Mark as principal of St. Joseph High School in 1975, and succeeded Fr. Mark as Pastor.

In February 2002, Sr. Catherine Sullivan, DMJ, joined the parish staff as the Pastoral Assistant, continuing again the close working relationship between the Josephites and Daughters of Mary and Joseph here in Santa Maria. In prior years, during the time of Fr. Garcia's tenure, Sr. Linda Webb, DMJ, worked in the parish.

MORE RECENT EVENTS AND ACTIVITIES

As the Orcutt area has continued to grow, so have the offerings of the school and parish. The school now has Kindergarten, and a computer lab. The parish constructed a "gathering area" adjoining the Church and it was first used on Palm Sunday, 2003.

During 2003, St. Louis de Montfort commemorated 40 years of growth. Parishioners came together to remember their history and to honor those whose dedication helped make St. Louis de Montfort a living community of faith.

On April 3, 2011, hundreds of people gathered following Mass to celebrate and dedicate a new 6,000 square foot building. This beautiful two-story addition replaced the 25-year-old temporary modular buildings that were shared by many parish ministries.

Regional Bishop Thomas Curry conducted the Mass and celebrated the dedication ceremony with Santa Barbara County 4th District Supervisor Joni Gray, building architect Jorge Machin, builder Joe Halsell and construction foreman Rick Biely.

The Hispanic ministry provided a taco lunch for the celebration. Pastor Charles Hofschulte said the dedication was a culmination of a three-year fundraising and a nine-month building effort.

ST. LOUIS DE MONTFORT OUTREACH MINISTRIES

The SHINE Retreat
The SEARCH Retreat

CAFÉ (Catholic Adult Formation and Education)
Boy Scouts and Cub Scouts
Girl Scouts
Juvenile Detention Ministry
Homeless Shelter Services
Knights of Columbus
Food Pantry

ST. LOUIS DE MONTFORT PASTORAL STAFF

Rev.Charles Hofschulte, CJ: Pastor (frcharles@sldm.org)
Rev. Alidor Mikobi, CJ: In residence (mikobiali@yahoo.fr)
Rev. John Mayhew, CJ: Associate (Hispanic Ministry)
Rev. L. Mark Newman, CJ: Associate

St. Louis, as "One Family in Christ" will continue to meet the needs of the growing community.

ST. LOUIS DE MONTFORT CATHOLIC CHURCH
1190 East Clark Avenue
Santa Maria, California 93455
(805) 937-4555

Mass   Schedule

St. Louis de Montfort:

Sunday:	7:30, 9:30, 11:30 AM and 6:00 PM
Saturday:	8:00 AM, 5:30 & 6:45 PM (Spanish Mass)
Daily:	6:30 & 8:00 AM
Holy Day Masses:	6:30, 8:00, 9:30 AM and 6:00 PM
Eve of Holy Day"	5:30 & 6:45 PM (Spanish Mass)
First Fridays/Lent & Advent	6:30 & 8:00 AM and 5:30 PM
Rosary:	7:30 AM Daily
Confessions:	Saturday 3:30-5:00 & 8:00-9:00 PM (Spanish and English); Thursday before First Fridays 7:30 PM
Baptisms:	By appointment and after instruction only. Please call the rectory for more information.
Weddings:	By appointment only. The date may not be fixed until after consultation with a priest from the parish. Please call the rectory.

Adoration of Blessed Sacrament: All night adoration 7:00 PM Thursdays before First Friday until 6:00 AM Friday. Sign up board available at least one week prior.

Novena of Our Lady of Perpetual Help: Thursday at 7:00 PM

San Ramon Chapel (Sisquoc):   Sunday Mass: 10:15 AM

St. Anthony's (Los Alamos):   Sunday Mass: 8:45 AM (English) 11:30 AM (Spanish)

CHAPTER TWENTY

ST. ANDREW UNITED METHODIST

EARLY HISTORY

In 1962, twenty-five families set out from First United Methodist Church downtown to share the good news of Jesus Christ, and start a new church in the growing southern end of the Santa Maria Valley.

The Bishop of the Southern California-Arizona Annual Conference of the United Methodist Church appointed Mike Winstead as pastor.

A committee was formed and met in September 1962, at the former parsonage. One of the actions was to agree on the name of the church. Since no other church had so honored St. Andrew, that name was chosen.

Sunday, October 14, 1962, was the first worship service. It was held in an old roller rink called TOM-DOM ROLLERDOME, which was located near the intersection of Orcutt Expressway and Airport Way. The facility was rented from the Santa Maria Airport District for part of the building for $35 per month. This old building was an idle place for skunks, and even the bees swarmed and tried to make a new hive in the rafters! All the youth loved the place with its freedom to explore, and the adults never fussed at them to keep it spotless.

January 20, 1963, was the official organizational chartering date, followed by an all-church potluck and celebration. Attending this celebration were 113 charter members.

Everyone worked. Everyone cleaned. Everyone grew in Christian love and fellowship. They became one family, helping and caring for each other, and the bond has remained strong over the years.

The current sanctuary was built in 1990 and an administrative wing was added to it in 1998. St. Andrew United Methodist Church is now debt-free.

St. Andrew has become very active in the community, chartering, organizing and sponsoring both the Happy Hollow Preschool and the St. Andrew Academy of Music.

Prayer, praise, worship, fellowship, education and service are all vital ministries at St. Andrew. You will find a warm welcome awaiting you, inviting you to join with them and walk in faith together.

ST. ANDREW ACADEMY OF MUSIC

The Academy of Music opened its doors on March 1, 1999.   Pastor Al Jansen came to St. Andrew in 1994 and brought with him the idea of a music academy.   The goal of the music academy is to offer musical instruction to students in the Santa Maria Valley.

Music is a universal language.   Music involves family and community participation at home, at school, and at church.

Teaching music at the Academy is both a great joy and a challenge.   Music reaches all children, and the Academy takes great delight in helping students develop their abilities.

Melody Jones is the Executive Director of the academy who oversees the administrative functions.   Various teachers do the actual teaching.

THE BELLS OF ST. ANDREW

St. Andrew is well-known for its hand bell choir, which was formed in 1991 and is still active today, under the leadership of Scott Davis.

OUTREACH

St. Andrew United Methodist Church supports, through our denomination, thousands of mission centers and projects in America and throughout the world.

As a congregation, we support the Good Samaritan Homeless Shelter by preparing and serving meals on the 4th Saturday of each month, and take a canned food offering on Communion Sundays to support our in-house food pantry.

St. Andrew directly supports four missionaries around the world who include Luis Aramayo and Eunice Arias in Venezuela, Terry Henderson in Mexico, and the Siberia-Far East District.

St. Andrew sponsors an Alternative Gift Market at the Christmas season to give people the opportunity to purchase life-enriching gifts for the needy people and areas around the globe.

Through the Church's Almoner's Fund, monies are collected to be used, at the Pastor's discretion, for those who come to the church seeking assistance.

St. Andrew also sponsors the Santa Maria Crop Walk against world hunger, which raises funds to feed the hungry, both on the Central Coast and worldwide.

OTHER COMMUNITY INVOLVEMENT

St. Andrew has long been involved with: Camp Arroyo Grande; United Methodist Women; United Methodist Men; Good Samaritan Shelter; Food Bank; Boy Scouts; Girl Scouts.

The church allows the Orcutt Youth Football to utilize their field. And St. Andrew has had a long-standing rapport with their neighbor, Righetti High School.

The current pastor (since 2009) is Reverend David Camphouse. He is married to Anna, and they have a young daughter, Sophia. Reverend David brings a youthful vitality to the church.

ST. ANDREW UNITED METHODIST CHURCH
3945 South Bradley Road
Santa Maria, California 93455
(805) 937-2470

OUR MISSION:
To serve God by sharing, teaching and living the Word

OUR VISION:
Build disciples, grow in faith, and serve in Christ's name

SUNDAY WORSHIP

8:30 AM: Praise Service
10:20 AM: Traditional Service

CHAPTER TWENTY-ONE

PINE GROVE BAPTIST CHURCH

Pine Grove Baptist is a result of the vision of the people of First Baptist Church of Santa Maria. In the early 1960s, the population of the entire Santa Maria Valley was exploding. First Baptist Church completed a spacious new auditorium at Fesler and Vine, yet found itself crowded. The vision was cast for a daughter church in the Orcutt area that would become the home of many of the Orcutt residents who were members of the First Baptist Church.

The vision took shape when, on August 15, 1962, First Baptist Church voted to purchase two+ acres of land at the corner of Bradley and Rice Ranch Roads for the price of $23,000. It was the site of the original Pine Grove School.

Sunday School classes began in the residence that was on the property. Groundbreaking for the first building project took place on November 3, 1963. The two-story educational building of 7,200 square feet was built for $65,000. The first services were held in the building on October 18, 1964. A dedication service was held Sunday, April 11, 1965.

The ministry of Pastor Harlan Rahilly, his wife Harriet, and their daughters Sharon and Sandra, began on September 7, 1964. They served the church until the middle of 1969. Under his leadership, the process of organizing as a local church was completed on December 28, 1964. Charter membership was open from December 28, 1964 to March 31,1965. Fifty-three people signed that charter.

Children's and youth ministries have always been a major emphasis of Pine Grove Baptist Church. One example is the AWANA program, which began in 1966. Hundreds of area children and teens have participated in this still-vibrant ministry.

The tenure of Pastor Glen Golike, along with his wife Judy and three sons, Gary, Scott, and Dale, began on January 4, 1970. Pastor Golike led the church in some major advances during his twenty years of ministry at the church. On October 14, 1970, the church became independent from First Baptist Church, in accordance with the original plan of both groups.

After seeking the right financing for over a year, the church voted to secure a loan from Mid-State Bank for $135,000, with a fifteen year payoff. Groundbreaking for the building of 7,500 square feet, with seating for 400 in the sanctuary, was held on June 17, 1973. The first service in the new building was on February 10, 1974. The Dedication Service was held on March 15, 1974. The final payment on the mortgage was made on December 1, 1988. A mortgage burning celebration was held on January 29, 1989.

On August 27, 1975, the church voted to proceed with the purchase of one acre of land west of the church for $30,000. This Rice Ranch Road property included a house and two garages.

A ministry to senior citizens, known as Golden Years Fellowship, was begun by Bert and Dena DeKorte and Ralph and Catherine McIntyre on June 15, 1979 and continues to this day.

On May 27, 1990, the church voted to call Bruce McLain to serve as pastor. June 24, 1990, was the first Sunday for Pastor McLain, his wife Margie, and their three children, Steven, Laura, and Katie. During Pastor McLain's ministry, which has now exceeded twenty-one years at the church, major improvements have been made to the church facilities. There have also been new programs for leadership training, men's and women's ministries, an expansion of the music ministry, a community-sponsored Easter Egg Hunt, a Halloween carnival for the neighborhood, known as Trunk or Treat, a home school program, and other ministries to build up the church and minister to the community.

Several men have served alongside the pastors including: George Hough, who served from 1975 to 1977; D.J. Bayne in 1979; Mark Lixey from 1983 to 1984, and again from 1986 to 2004; Dick Parker in 1983; and Tim Farley from 2006 to 2009.

The church has always had a strong interest in world missions and has commissioned several of its members for service around the world, including: Betty DeVoe Dion in 1975 for missionary service in Brazil; David and Dennise Rhoads for service in Papua New Guinea in 2003; Laura McLain for service in Portugal in 2009; and Evandro and Erica da Silvia who serve in Brazil in 2009.

Pine Grove Baptist continues to fulfill its vision, which is summarized in four statements:

1. We exist to glorify God:
EXALTATION OF GOD

2. We exist to build up God's people:
EDIFICATION OF GOD'S PEOPLE

3. We exist to reach our community with the gospel of Jesus Christ:
ESTABLISHMENT IN THE COMMUNITY

4. We exist to be involved in the evangelization of the world:
EVANGELISM THROUGHOUT THE WORLD

PINE GROVE BAPTIST CHURCH
5551 South Bradley Road
P.O. Box 2088
Santa Maria, California 93457
(805) 937-4538
Website: www.PineGroveBaptistChurchSM.org
Email: PineGroveBaptist@verizon.net

SCHEDULE OF SERVICES

Sunday
Sunday School: 9:30 AM
Worship Services: 10:50 AM
6:00 PM

Awana Clubs: 6:00 – 7:45 PM
(During the school year)

Nursery care provided for all services.

Other ministries as scheduled.

CHAPTER TWENTY-TWO

TEMPLE BETH EL

Although Temple Beth El wasn't dedicated until June 1, 1969, there is a long history of Jewish people and their positive influence and contributions in the Santa Maria area decades before that time.

World War II and Camp Cooke brought military personnel, which included Jewish families, to the Santa Maria area. Many stayed or returned after the end of World War II.

With no synagogue in Santa Maria, the Jewish families met in private homes, social clubs, or wherever they could. One comment in Beth El's history records reads: "The High Holidays were held in various locations but mostly at the Methodist Church. They were very cooperative." This remark is further borne out by a Methodist hymnal in the First United Methodist Church archives which is inscribed inside the front cover: "This hymn book has been presented to the church by Temple Beth El in honor of friendship."

The first formal organization of Jews was named the "Amity Club" (which means Friendship) and was established in 1954.

One of the first needs of the early congregation was to purchase a Torah, a parchment scroll containing the first five books of the Bible, known in Judaism as "The Five Books of Moses." Fund-raising began in 1957 to fulfill this need.

The Articles of Incorporation were implemented February 28, 1964.

At a meeting in January 1964, the Temple voted to purchase one and two-thirds acres on East Alvin Street for $12,500.

Construction of the Temple at 1501 E. Alvin was a long and arduous road, one filled with countless hours of volunteer labor. The formal dedication was Sunday, June 1, 1969, at 1 p.m. David Seigel of Encino, vice-president of the Pacific Southwest Council, Union of American Hebrew Congregations, delivered the dedication address. Representing Santa Maria was Mayor George Hobbs, while Rev. Stanley Smith represented the Santa Maria Ministerial Assn. Music was provided by Von and Rex Gallion.

TEMPLE BETH EL.
The formal dedication of Temple Beth El was on June 1, 1969.

For the next several decades Temple Beth El continued to grow in membership, establishing a religious school and conducting bar and bat mitzvahs.

The temple has remained a center for Jewish life in the Santa Maria Valley. It celebrates major Jewish holidays including Rosh Hashanah (New Year), Yom Kippur (Day of Atonement), Sukkot, Simchat Torah, Purim and Passover. For many years, the annual Hanukkah Party and Raffle has been a major fund-raiser for the temple.

Religious and lay leaders conduct Friday evening Sabbath services, followed by an "oneg," or social hour, usually hosted by a member who is recognizing a memorial or personal event such as a birthday or anniversary. There are Torah study sessions on two Saturday mornings each month.

Temple Beth El continues its tradition of hosting cultural, social and entertainment events such as:

A seminar discussion on the changing meaning of Zionism

A Purim "Fun Fest and Fund Raiser" with comedian Keith Barany

"A Mideast Update" by Randy Neal, regional director, Christians United for Israel
A presentation by Maggie Anton, author of "Rashi's Daughters"
Opera Night at Temple Beth El -- Puccini's "Tosca"
"From Broadway to Bluegrass" with Diane Borad-Mirken and the Wild
    River Ramblers

On May 22, 2011, Temple Beth El hosted a concert entitled "Musical Sunday -- Americana and Bluegrass" where widely known musicians showcased their talents. On June 26, 2011, the temple will "Celebrate the American Musical" featuring song-and-dance man Gale McNeeley and pianist Betty Faas. For many years, the temple's families have celebrated July 4th with a festive BBQ on the back lawn.

Temple Beth El continues to serve the Santa Maria Valley's Jewish population in three important ways--as a house of worship, a house of study and a house of community.

TEMPLE BETH EL
1501 East Alvin
P.O. Box 5217
Santa Maria, California 93456
(805) 928-2118
Email: TempleBethEl@verizon.net

CHAPTER TWENTY-THREE

VICTORY HARVEST CHURCH OF GOD IN CHRIST
(FORMERLY JOHNSON TEMPLE)
(It is still Johnson Temple Outreach Program)

Although they first met in facilities in Guadalupe and Nipomo, Johnson Temple was not officially established in Santa Maria until their building at 619 North Railroad was dedicated April 22, 1973.

Originally named Johnson Temple after its founder, Rev. Orie Johnson, the name was later changed to Victory Harvest. Many people still refer to it as "Johnson Temple." Orie is still the pastor to this day. His wife, Sister Gladys Johnson is a real "shaker and mover" in getting things done.

The church building was built with considerable community volunteer labor.

Other churches, especially the Baptist and the Mormon churches, lent much assistance to get this church started. The Mormons were particularly helpful in dealing with matters with the City of Santa Maria.

One of the truly impressive community service programs they perform is to provide sacks of commodities to families in need every third Monday morning of the month. Sometimes, more than 200 people will show up to receive food, with most of the food provided by the local Food Bank.

Before the Food Bank came into existence in Santa Maria, Orie and members of the congregation had to take a van down to Santa Barbara to pick up the food! Then they went to the local grocery stores (Scolari, Lucky, Williams Brothers, Safeway) where they

VICTORY HARVEST CHURCH OF GOD IN CHRIST.
Dedicated on April 22, 1973.

picked up day-old bakery items to add to the food distribution. In addition to distributing the food at the church, they delivered food to nursing homes, low-rent apartments, and the parks. Gladys recalls how the people would come running when the van pulled into the parks!

Sister Gladys Johnson oversees the packing and organizing of brown bags of food for distribution. After so many years of doing this, the volunteers function as a well-organized team.

In addition to the above-mentioned food distribution activities, the Senior Brown Bag Program gives out sacks of commodities at Victory Harvest Church every other Thursday of the month.

The church rents out their facilities for community activities for income.

The Johnsons couldn't recall the exact dates (they thought it was around 1990), Dr. Ruth Rogers from Hancock College conducted literacy classes at Victory Harvest Church. And, currently, computer classes are held there twice a week.

Two of their fundraising events conducted by the church are the Fourth of July fireworks sales, and the barbeques, which are usually held in their parking lot. These events provide much-needed income for the church.

One of the Elders of the church also has a prison ministry program.

REV. ORIE AND GLADYS JOHNSON.
Founder and Leaders of the Victory Harvest Church of God in Christ, in Santa Maria.

Although not the oldest Afro-American church in Santa Maria, Orie Johnson currently holds the record as being the oldest active minister (82 years young), who is still the pastor of the church he founded 38 years ago.   His keen mind and his tall, lanky build make it hard to believe he is 82 years of age!

Prayer requests are desired for Orie's wife, Gladys, who is going through a rough time following recent surgery for cancer.

VICTORY HARVEST SUNDAY SERVICES
Sunday School - 9:30 A.M.
Morning Worship - 11:00 A.M.
Spanish-speaking Worship (this service recently added) - 5:00 P.M.

A warm welcome is extended to one and all!   You may even hear some of the old favorite hymns such as "When the Roll is Called up Yonder I'll be There."

VICTORY HARVEST CHURCH OF GOD IN CHRIST
(Formerly Johnson Temple)
619 North Railroad
Santa Maria, California
(805) 922-3042

CHAPTER TWENTY-FOUR

ST. JOHN NEUMANN CATHOLIC CHURCH

St. John Neumann's history is a bit unusual. The church first operated as a satellite of St. Mary's then was split off on February 1, 1986 into its own parish. Father Herrera was the parish priest and was very involved in its establishment, and in construction of the church. Father Herrera was promoted to Monsignor in 1999.

Then, in 2001, Monsignor Herrera was reassigned to St. Amydius Church in Lynwood.

As of July 1, 2011, Monsignor Herrera is back with St. John Neumann. Also effective July 1, 2011, Father Rolando Sierra from St. Gertrude Catholic Church in Bell Gardens was assigned to St. John Neumann.

St. John Neumann has experienced considerable growth over the years and has expanded its ministry. The Church is very actively involved in the Filipino Catholic community, in which they have their Santo Nino Novena on Fridays at 5:00 PM. There are Choirs in English and Spanish at both Sunday Masses, where music, which speaks to the heart in any language, is an important part of St. John Neumann's services.

Monsignor Herrera is very excited about continuing his ministry here in Santa Maria. There is so much work to be done, as there are around 7,000 registered Catholic families in his parish. And these are tough times for the struggling families. There is never enough food or money. But it is important to keep a deep faith and signs of hope for the future, and to instill a love for the Lord.

The food pantry at the church is always in need of nonperishable food, especially rice, beans and canned goods. Donations to help those in need can be dropped off at the Rectory.

Attendance is very good at the Masses. Let us all pray that better economic times are on the horizon.

Nancy Dort is in charge of the church's participation in the ministry at the Good Samaritan Shelter.

February 1, 2011, marked the 25th Anniversary of the establishment of St. John Neumann parish. May God bless them as they work to further God's Kingdom in Santa Maria.

MASS SCHEDULE

English Masses
Sundays: 7:00 AM; 10:30 AM; 5:00 PM
Tuesdays and Thursdays: 8:00 AM

Misas en Espanol
Sabados: 7:00 pm
Domingos: 8:30 AM; 12:30 PM; 2:30 PM; 7:00 PM
Lunes, Miercoles, Viernes, Sabado, 8:00 AM

Confessions/Confesiones
Saturdays/Sabados: 4:00 PM – 6:00 PM
Thursdays, 7:00 PM – 8:00 PM

ST. JOHN NEUMANN CATHOLIC CHURCH
966 West Orchard Street
Santa Maria, California 93458-2063
Phone: (805) 922-7099   FAX: (805) 346-1747
Email: st.neumann@stneumann.com

CHAPTER TWENTY-FIVE

ORTHODOX CHURCH OF THE ANNUNCIATION

The miraculous formation of the Orthodox Church of the Annunciation was initiated by Mr. John Warren in 1979. Mr. Warren, a former choir director at Holy Virgin Mary Cathedral, Los Angeles, began contacting Orthodox families on the Central Coast and bringing them together for the purpose of founding a mission. That summer, the group sent a petition to Fr. Thaddeus Wojcik, the Dean of the Pacific Southwest Deanery, requesting recognition by the Orthodox Church in America. By fall, Father Ian MacKinnon, a newly ordained priest and recent graduate of St. Vladimir's Orthodox Theological Seminary, was appointed rector of the fledgling community by Metropolitan THEODOSIUS. He and his wife, Nina, moved to Santa Maria in December.

The initial group of fifteen families met at St. Peter's Episcopal church. The Divine Liturgy was not able to be served until the afternoon hours, after the parish's own weekly services were completed.

In the summer of 1980, the group found a better alternative in a vacant storage building behind the Marian Residence -- a Roman Catholic convalescent home for retired nuns of the Marian order. The local Roman Catholic bishop permitted the group to set up a permanent chapel in a building that had once been a part of Marian Hospital before it relocated and transformed the complex into a retirement facility. The director of the facility, Mother Barbara, gave her enthusiastic support to the work, setting rent at such a low rate ($25 per month) that the Residence was, no doubt, underwriting most of the associated costs.

During the next twenty-four years, this 700 square foot, two-room area was to be the home of Annunciation Mission. As the parish grew, several renovations were made to the chapel, including the addition of a 200 square foot narthex.

Though small, inconspicuous and rather poorly located, inestimable blessings and saving Mysteries were accomplished and celebrated in this space. At an Episcopal visit for the Feast of the Annunciation (March 25th), Bishop TIKHON once observed that this small Orthodox chapel was Santa Maria's focal point for the Divine Light that the angels of heaven behold during the Divine Services of the Church.

Father MacKinnon served the community until July of 1982, at which time Deacon Mark Kozak and his wife Jan arrived in Santa Maria. Father Deacon Mark continued to serve the community as a deacon until February of 1984, when he was ordained to the Holy Priesthood by Bishop GREGORY (Afonsky) of the Diocese of Alaska and assigned as acting rector. The ordination took place at the chapel, and more than 100 people attended. After laboring for three and a half years at Annunciation, Father Mark and Jan left the Mission, and Priest Mark was attached to St. Nicolas Church in Saratoga, California.

With the transfer of Father Mark, Father John Bernardi became the parish's temporary priest until August of 1986. Financial hardship forced the Bernardi family to relocate to Las Vegas, Nevada.

After Father John's departure, the parish was without a priest for a year. Periodically, Hiermonk Andre (Levshin), a retired priest living in the area, would come from San Luis Obispo and celebrate the Divine Liturgy. But most weeks the parish was without priestly services. However, the faithful remained steadfast, and continued to hold Reader Services and meet for fundraisers and social events. It is to the credit of some tenacious members that the parish survived during this period, for it would have been easy to disband.

In August of 1987, George Masters and his wife, Georgette, moved to Santa Maria from Holy Cross Greek Orthodox Seminary in Boston Shortly after his arrival, the seminary graduate was ordained to the Holy Priesthood by the newly consecrated hierarch, Vladyka TIKHON. The ordination took place at St. Herman Church in Oxnard, California. St. Herman's and Annunciation jointly hosted the reception afterward. Father George remained in Santa Maria for one year, and, in July 1988, he, like Father Mark before him, moved to Saratoga and was attached to St. Nicolas Church.

The four priests who served Annunciation from 1979 to 1988 all experienced a common difficulty: lack of financial support. All four were forced to seek out full-time employment in an area where housing costs are high and salary levels are comparatively low. All four families reported leaving the area in debt, having exhausted their personal resources. Rather than continue the same pattern, Bishop TIKHON decided to appoint Father Ian MacKennon (the parish's first rector) as priest-in-charge (July 1988). Father Ian enlisted the help of two priests living in driving distance, Father Luke Hill and Father David Ogan, and was able to provide the Mission with a weekly, Saturday Divine Liturgy. Father Ian made monthly visits to establish and raise a realistic salary package and conducted Vespers services, Bible Studies, and planning sessions.

After three critical years of planning and up-building, the community was ready to commit itself to another resident priest. Father Lawrence Russell, along with Matushka Cheryl and their two children, Stephen and Michelle, arrived in the summer of 1991. With the coming of some unpredicted growth to the Central Coast area and some economic stabilization in the work force, the Mission began to experience some long awaited numerical growth.

Much in need of the help of God, the parish received an unexpected and incalculable blessing when a portion of the relics of the Grand Duchess and new martyr Elizabeth was bestowed on the community through St. Barbara's Monastery (Santa Barbara). The icon which was painted at a monastery in Greece and the relics of the Saint have been a constant stream of Grace in the life of the parishioners. The parish's consolation and stewardship grew again when in August of 1998 the parish received a much-treasured portion of the relics of St. Herman of Alaska (bestowed by Metropolitan THEODOSIUS) and, again, when in May 2003 a portion of the newly-uncovered relics of the Russian, Venerable

Father, Gerasim, of Bolindo Monastery arrived on the eve of his commemoration. The relics of these saints are greatly revered by the community, "being more precious than the most exquisite jewels, and more purified than gold" (Martyrdom of St. Polycarp).

At the prayers of the Mother of God and the Saints, a most unexpected wonder occurred in January of 1997: Parishioner Edith Kaplan donated the capital necessary for the construction of a church and a social hall. Given the high cost of land and the size of the community, this donation brought into reach a hope that seemed little more than a pleasant dream. A perfect parcel of land was located and purchased. Ms. Kaplan took up residence in the house on the southwest corner of the property. Diocesan Architect John DellaMonica was contacted and some preliminary elevations were drawn for the construction of the buildings.

ORTHODOX CHURCH OF THE ANNUNCIATION.
*The Blessing of the New Temple on February 4, 2011, marked
31 years since the founding of the Santa Maria Church.*

In December of 2004, twenty-four years after Father Ian's arrival, phase one construction began. After seven months of toil and sacrifice, the community held its first Divine Liturgy in the new social hall. All agreed that it was according to Divine schedule that this service was held on August 1, the first day of the Dormition fast. No one dares believe that without the help of the Mother of God, we could have survived as a community.
The community recognizes that this property is a sacred entrustment. The leadership of the parish is busy working on how this new facility can be used to bring glory to God through works of mercy and fidelity to the Faith that we hold. We are grateful to God for

all He has done, to the Theotkos and the Saints for their intercessions and heavenly ministry and to each and every parishioner who has been a co-worker with God in this labor of love.

ORTHODOX CHURCH OF THE ANNUNCIATION
877 Francine Lane
Santa Maria, California 93456
(805) 938-7877

CHAPTER TWENTY-SIX

MT. ZION CHURCH OF GOD IN CHRIST

HISTORY

The church building at 419 West Fesler Street was originally the location of the Foursquare Church. They bought the land in 1929, built a church upon it, and resided there until they built a new church building at 709 North Curryer in 1959 and moved into it.

Foursquare Church sold their old building (419 West Fesler) to The Salvation Army who occupied it until they were able to purchase the old LDS (Mormon) Chapel at the corner of Cook and Miller Streets.

In 1970, Rev. Julius A. Ford, pastor of Mt. Zion Church of God in Christ, purchased the building at 419 West Fesler Street from The Salvation Army. He saved the condemned church building from demolition and repaired it with his own hands. The building is still home to Mt. Zion to this day.

MT. ZION CHURCH OF GOD IN CHRIST.
Purchased in 1970, this is now the church building for Mt. Zion.

Pastor Ford moved his family from Paso Robles in December 1968 but continued to commute to Paso Robles three days a week to preach at his old church there, while he established a ministry in Santa Maria. Until they bought the property at 419 West Fesler, they held church in rented space.

Like many pastors, especially in smaller churches, Rev. Ford has had to work numerous jobs to support his ministry. He and his wife, Betty, have seven children and have experienced much hardship to raise their family and keep the church active.

Mt. Zion experienced an explosion of growth during the 1970s, when Vandenberg was in a time of tremendous expansion. Pastor Ford was the Civilian Chaplain and was kept extremely busy. In those days, many Afro-American airmen, especially from the South, were looking for a local church. Mt. Zion reminded them of home, and attendance on weekends sometimes swelled to 300 persons.

For a relatively small church, Mt. Zion has an impressive Youth Choir. Participants are: Janae Marshae Sloan; Nahkyo Taylor; Nyasia Brown; Tia Jones; Cleve Jones; Alexie;

Cierrah Mack; Jada Ford; Victor Ford; Anja Ford; and Jasmine Ford. Many of these youth choir members are praise dancers as well. Praise dancer Nahkya Taylor, who performed in angel attire to music at the 41st Anniversary party on Sunday afternoon, August 7, 2011, was as graceful as a ballerina. In addition to the Youth Choir, Mt. Zion also has a wonderful Adult Choir, which really gets the church "rocking."

Geno Williams, Assistant Pastor, has started an outreach program in the community, which ministers to those people who are unable to attend church services – home-bound, people in hospitals or convalescent homes, etc.

August 4-7, 2011, Mt. Zion celebrated its 41st anniversary and Pastor Supt. Julius A. Ford and his wife, Missionary Betty J. Ford's 41st year of pastorship. It was a joyous occasion, with people attending from New Mexico, Las Vegas, Nevada, and Bakersfield. Other local churches in Santa Maria participated in the "grand finale" celebration on Sunday afternoon. Other choirs performed as well as their bands. There was a lady who played the saxophone who did an outstanding job, also a soloist with a golden voice.

SPANISH MINISTRY AT MT. ZION

Pastor Luis Nunez has been the minister for the Spanish services at Mt. Zion for over 20 years. Also a minister over Spanish services is Luis Prado. They have quite a good band: Francisco Hernandez Lopez on piano; Mario Leyeva on guitar; Fieliberto Assencion, soloist; Jose Cortez on drums, and Dimeccio Morales. Music speaks its own language and breaks down barriers, so non-Spanish-speakers are caught up in the beauty of the service.

Services in Spanish are held at the following times:
    Tuesday – 7:00 P.M.
    Thursday – 7:00 P.M.
    Sunday – 4:00 P.M.
    There is also a Spanish Bible Study on Saturdays.

Outreach activities within the Spanish community, and attendance at their services is good.

MT. ZION CHURCH OF GOD IN CHRIST
419 West Fesler Street
Santa Maria, California 93458
(805) 922-0700

CHAPTER TWENTY-SEVEN

FIRST CHURCH OF GOD

HISTORY

When Britt Fairchild, features writer for the Santa Maria Times, wrote an article in 2004 commemorating the 50th Anniversary of the First Church of God, at 613 North Elizabeth Street in Santa Maria, she said it, "has a heart of a congregation twice its size." That was seven years ago, but it still holds true today.

When the church began in 1954, only about a dozen or so members made up the congregation. They started out meeting in homes, then in rented space.

Then Estelle Lisech, who was the first pastor, and her husband, Frank, gave the small congregation a church they could be proud of. The couple, who came to Santa Maria in 1954 to start the Church of God here, purchased a house with an adjacent lot, on North Elizabeth Street.

Construction of the new church building began in 1956, with mostly volunteer labor, and was dedicated the following year. Subsequently, the Lisech's home was moved to another location in Santa Maria.

The pastoral roll, each building on the work done before them, is as follows:

Estelle Lisech, Church Planter, May 1954-1958
Emmett and Rita Hofer, 1958-1963
Lawrence and Lucille Durst, 1963-1965
Howard and Maria Leverett, 1965-1988
Steve and Marilyn McCoy, 1988-1998
Phil and Gail Canipe, 1999-Present

Pastor Phil Canipe, who has been the pastor since 1999, has high praise for his congregation. The church stretches through generations, and there is a spirit of unity among members. The small size of the church, and its residential location, is a challenge for further growth, but, as Pastor Canipe says, "I think God is at work in churches of all sizes."

EVANGELIZATION

The Church of God has always had a strong emphasis on world evangelization. They provide prayer and financial support for these efforts through their headquarters in Anderson, Indiana, including efforts in the central part of California and locally.

111

The Church of God also provides assistance to other ministries not associated with their church:

Care-Net Crisis Pregnancy Center: Provides some monthly support to Care-Net Crisis Pregnancy Center. This ministry provides support and alternatives to women considering abortion.

Samaritan Shelter: A group from First Church of God is there monthly to provide and serve a meal to the residents.

MAJOR CONCERNS (in Pastor Phil's own words):

"**The Ethical and Moral Disintegration of our Nation.** We believe the only way to restore America to her former greatness is through a spiritual revival in our churches. This will only occur as we prayerfully wait on God and allow Him to change our hearts. As multitudes of people are transformed and begin to have a renewed concern to live in a way that honors God, and expresses love and respect for every human being, our culture will be renewed. America will be changed one heart at a time. We believe the message of Jesus Christ is the only means for this renewal.

"**Evangelism Primarily Through the Members of the Church, Apart from the Church Building.** While an increasing number of America's churches have begun to focus on attracting unbelievers to Sunday morning worship, using entertainment and other approaches that appeal to our culture, we are committed to following the New Testament model of church life. Worship, in our church, is geared primarily to edifying Christians and evangelism is done outside the church. Most new converts to Christ have a desire to connect with the church of the one who led them to the Lord. We won't have to compel them to come or allow the culture to shape the church's approach. We believe it is becoming increasingly clear that the church has made a profound mistake by becoming "market-driven." It completely misrepresents the message of Scripture and it has resulted in professing Christians who make little or no difference in our culture.

"**Marriage and Family.** America's homes are in disarray. We have a great concern that the home is disintegrating and that those who describe themselves as Christians have a similar divorce rate as the world. We believe the children of these couples are the ones who suffer the most. As the church begins to be renewed, this will begin to change, one family at a time."

SCHEDULE OF SERVICES

Sunday: 10:00 AM Worship
Monday: 6:30 PM New Life Course
Tuesday: 7:00 PM   Youth Ministry
Wednesday: 7:00 PM AWANA (kids age 4 to Grade 6)

FIRST CHURCH OF GOD
613 North Elizabeth Street
Santa Maria, California 93458
(805) 925-7933

CHAPTER TWENTY-EIGHT

CALVARY CHAPEL
(Non-Denominational)

HISTORY

Calvary Chapel was incorporated in March 1986. They first met in homes, then in the Seventh-day Adventist Church. Then, for a time, they rented the hall of the YMCA.

In 1991, they were finally able to rent space of their own in an industrial condo on McCoy Lane. That first condo was only 2400 square feet. They kept expanding on McCoy from 2400 SF, then 4800 SF, then 6200 SF, then 8400 SF. Even that space became too small, so they began looking for a large building of their own to buy.

The old Grossman building supply and hardware store on Santa Maria Way became vacant. It sat vacant for several years and fell into an even worse state of disrepair. Bechtel Corporation became the owner of a number of Grossman holdings.

Pastor Paul Berry and Jerry Schmidt (a Commercial Realtor) flew to San Francisco and met with the CEO of Bechtel. They were able to negotiate a contract to buy the old building and the 5 acres of land for $860,000 in 1998.

The building was a mess. It had been rented at Halloween a time or two for a Haunted House. Vagrants and homeless had often "camped out" there. But it contained 30,000 square feet of space "under roof", which made it ideal size-wise. The rebuilding of the structure took two years. On November 11, 2001, Calvary Chapel finally got a Certificate of Occupancy. After all the volunteer labor, headaches, etc., they finally had a "home of their own." They also ended up with a hefty mortgage!

At that time, the church had a congregation of 35 people (which included Pastor Berry, his wife, and their two children). Now it has grown to where it has over 1,000 people in its congregation.

MINISTRIES, PROGRAMS AND ACTIVITIES

Calvary Chapel now also has several Assistant Ministers to help Pastor Berry. They are:

Terry Evans, Children's Minister
Neil Cunningham, Senior High Youth Minister
Mark Arkinson, Junior High Youth Minister

Tony Guy, Couples Minister and Marriage Counselor
Janet Villarete, SPEEDERS (+55) Minister
Ashley Crothers, Worship Minister

Calvary Chapel has "planted" several churches, all of which are self-supporting, in the following locations:

Bristol, England
Vandenberg Village, Lompoc, CA
Guadalupe, CA
Nipomo, CA

The church operates a Preschool year-round.   They conduct a Vacation Bible School once a year in the summer.

THE STORY OF THE TRUST HOME   (Tibetan Refugee Unreached Salvable Tribe)

The following story is unique to Calvary Chapel, and is, indeed, a beautiful one that deserves to be told.

Dolma and Arjun are a beautiful Christian couple, whom the Lord has blessed with a ministry to the poorest of the Tibetan children in Pokhara, Nepal.   Dolma is a Tibetan woman, who was carried on her mother's back out of Tibet to a refugee camp in Nepal. While in the camp, Dolma contracted tuberculosis.   She was treated by a Christian medical team and was led to the Lord by that team.   Arjun is a Nepali engineer.   He became a Christian when he saw the changes in Dolma.   Together they have one daughter and two beautiful grandchildren.

In 1995, Dolma felt that the Lord was calling them to start a ministry in Pokhara working in the Tibetan refugee camps.   This was a major move for them, and after much prayer and hard work the TRUST home was started with three children.   They now have over 70 children.

This is not an orphanage, but a true home for the children.   Dolma and Arjun consider each child a son or daughter.   They are very careful about selecting children for the home, and they pray over each one.   The children have rooms with four or five children in each room.   They mix the ages so the older children care for the younger ones.   They have devotions and prayer every morning and evening.   All the children attend the school on the grounds of the Home.

The main things we are praying for the Trust Home are:
1.   The spiritual growth of each child, particularly a strong foundation in the faith.
2.   Physical needs of the children.
3.   The health of Dolma and Argun.

4.   Wisdom, as many of the children are graduating from High School and are choosing careers.   Several are in training to take over the running of the Trust Home, so we are praying that the Lord will raise up the next generation of leadership for the Trust Home.

The TRUST Home Tibetan Children in Pokhara, Nepal.
Below is a picture of the children taken in 2010 by the Calvary Chapel team who traveled to Nepal to minister to the needs of the Trust Home.

CALVARY CHAPEL
(Non-Denominational)
2620 Santa Maria Way
Santa Maria, California 93455
(805) 922-1822

SENIOR PASTOR: Paul Berry

SERVICE TIMES

Sundays, 8:30 & 10:30 AM
Wednesdays, 7:00 PM

CHAPTER TWENTY-NINE

BETHEL KOREAN UNITED METHODIST

The ethnic and cultural composition of Santa Maria has changed considerably over the past decade. The historic old First United Methodist Church in the downtown mall has adapted to accommodate those changes.

Although Bethel Korean is not one of the historic old churches, it shares the use of the facilities of the historic old First United Methodist Church, so it is incorporated into this book. It is one of the four churches in Santa Maria chartered under the "UNITED" Methodist umbrella. The other three are: First United; Christ United; and St. Andrews United.

Since Bethel Korean United Methodist had no facilities of their own, on October 1, 2000, First United welcomed them to share use of their facilities.

On March 18, 2001, at 5:00 P.M. the Chartering Service for this newest United Methodist Church took place in the sanctuary at 311 South Broadway. "Beautiful" doesn't even begin to describe the service.

CHOIR, BETHEL KOREAN UNITED METHODIST CHURCH.
On March 18, 2001, the choir performed in traditional attire at its chartering celebration.

Rev. Paul Cheong, Minister of Bethel Korean UMC, gave the words of welcome. The opening hymn sung by everyone was so appropriate -- "The Church's One Foundation".

Choirs from three different Korean Churches (in traditional attire), from as far away as Zion Korean United Methodist Church in Los Angeles, traveled to Santa Maria to be a part of the service. Aurora Korean Church of Santa Maria presented special music.

Rev. Cheol H. Kwak, Santa Ana District Superintendent, Cal-Pac Conference, presented the sermon. Rev. Tom Heslop, Pastor, First United Methodist, read the scripture. Rev. Rich Garner, Santa Barbara District Superintendent presented the words of congratulations and encouragement.

Church services are at 1:00 P.M. Sundays, in the Sanctuary at 311 South Broadway.

WELCOME!

BETHEL KOREAN UNITED METHODIST
311 South Broadway
Santa Maria, California   93454-5105

CHAPTER THIRTY

FILIPINO CHRISTIAN CHURCH

This small church actually started more than twenty years ago as a mission work for Filipinos of the Iglesia Bautista Gethsemane.

The current pastor, Luke Martinez, came to Santa Maria on a mission trip from the Philippines in 1988, at the request of Pastor Juan Tobias. At that time, the church was Iglesia Bautista Gethsemane.

Pastor Luke Martinez returned to the Philippines, but on July 19, 1989, Pastor Juan Tobias asked him to return to Santa Maria on a permanent basis and join together with him in the ministry of the church.

Since Luke Martinez wasn't a Spanish-speaking minister, his sermons had to be translated from English to Spanish with Juan Tobias interpreting.

Then in 1990, Pastor Juan Tobias, who was suffering from poor health, returned to Texas. The church became a part of the Southern Baptist Conference and remains so today.

Pastor Luke, his wife Romelia, and their three children have worked hard over the years to build a place of worship, where all races and ages feel welcome.

Music is an important part of this ministry, where all ages participate in the music ministry. Piano, guitars, drums and voices blend together to worship God. Youth, seniors, women and men are encouraged to be active and provide input into the musical portion of the service.

Pastor Luke's vision for this church is for the people to grow in the life which God has given them, without compromising their faith. People need to witness and stand firm for what they believe. He believes in attracting people, not by "star power" or entertainment, but by the Word of God.

Small churches play an important role in Santa Maria. For many, they provide more of a sense of community and neighborhood.

FILIPINO CHRISTIAN CHURCH
410 West Church Street
Santa Maria, California   93458
(805) 714-6190

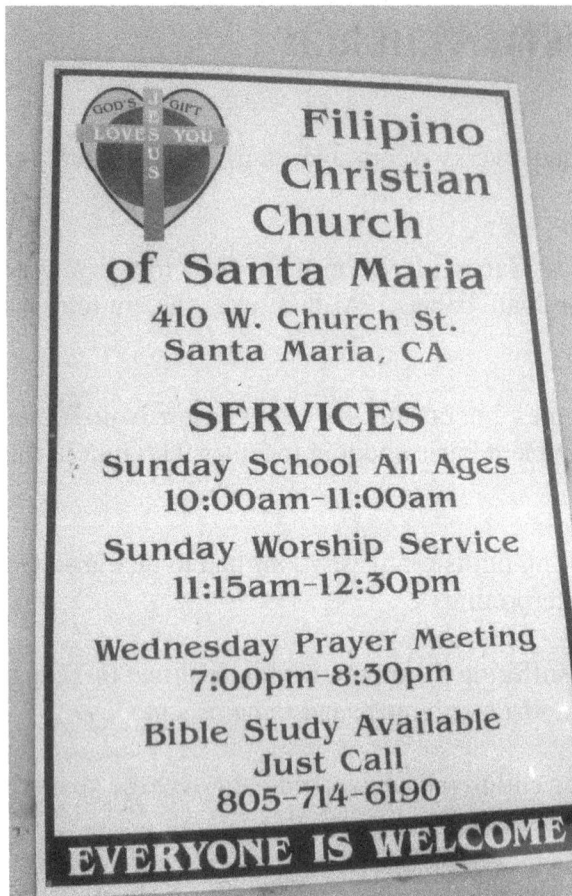

Welcome!

FILIPINO CHRISTIAN CHURCH
410 West Church Street
Santa Maria, California 93458
(805) 714-6190

CHAPTER THIRTY-ONE

NEW HOPE MISSIONARY BAPTIST CHURCH

HISTORY

November 20, 2011 marks the 50th Anniversary of New Hope Missionary Baptist Church. A big celebration is planned for this momentous occasion.

In November 1961, the New Hope Missionary Baptist Church was organized in the home of Brother Lwellyn and Sister Zetha Crow, in Nipomo, California. Dr. P. B. Mdodona became pastor at that time. Volunteer workers from St. Luke, Mt. Zion, and St. Paul Missionary Baptist churches assisted in this great event. The organizers of New Hope were: Lwellyn and Zetha Crow, Brother Carter, Steve and Sally Wilson, Francis Green (church clerk), Bertie Mae Hamilton, Meryl Berry (church treasurer), Melvin Robinson, Willie Pearl Mdodona (wife of the pastor) and children, Phyllis Lovaretta (pianist) and baby brother Crow. Organizing members Sister Bertie Mae Hamilton-Howard (December 2005) and Deacon Steve Wilson (March 2006) have gone on to be with our Lord.

After New Hope was organized, the church did not have a permanent place to worship. New Hope Missionary Baptist Church moved seven different times until the property located at 416 West Mill Street in Santa Maria was purchased under the leadership of Pastor W. R. Erwin. He became pastor of New Hope on December 19, 1968, and his wife, Sister Winifred Erwin became First Lady. Pastor Erwin served New Hope until his death in 1989. At that time, Dr. Earl E. James became the pastor. Pastor James, along with his wife First Lady Sydney James worked very hard overseeing the ministries of the church.

As a result of the vision of Pastor James, forty-five hundred square feet was added to the church, which includes the sanctuary, pastor's study, church office, kitchen, two restrooms, and the foyer. The old sanctuary was converted into the Erwin multi-purpose room/fellowship hall, which also serves as a place for Sunday school class, children's church, youth Bible study, and meeting rooms.

REVEREND HENRY L. LEWIS, JR.
AND SISTER AGATHA LEWIS.

On September 2, 2006, after 17 years of faithful service as the pastor of New Hope Missionary Baptist Church, Pastor James retired, turning the reins over to then Pastor Henry L. Lewis, Jr.

Pastor Henry L. Lewis, Jr. and Sister Agatha Shorter Lewis celebrated their first year as Pastor and First Lady of New Hope Missionary Baptist Church on August 24, 2007. During his first year as pastor, the church embraced the vision Pastor Lewis had of a family ministry: THE FAMILY THAT NOT ONLY PRAYS TOGETHER, STAYS TOGETHER. The family that studies the word of God together makes it a part of their lifestyle. These are the realities of a Christ-centered family.

REVEREND LEWIS AND
ASSOCIATE PASTOR ANTHONY KING

Pastor Lewis is truly equipping and empowering the family.

The church celebrated the burning of their mortgage on November 11, 2001. They also celebrated the purchase of the property located at 406 West Mill Street, located adjacent to the church, for future church expansion.

The New Hope members are actively involved in the Coast Counties Missionary Baptist District Association, the California State Baptist Convention, and the National Baptist Convention, USA, Inc.

MINISTRIES

Feeding the Homeless: Members of New Hope (some members of the choir, mission, and brotherhood) provide the food and feed the homeless at the Good Samaritan's Family Transitional and Emergency Shelters on the first Monday of each month. They were asked by the shelter officials, and agreed to extend this service on Thanksgiving Day.

The Women's Ministry: Mission meetings are held on the second and third Tuesday of each month. The Bible, and the National Mission Study Guide are the main sources of study. This department prepares food baskets during the holiday season for the needy families in the Santa Maria Valley. They also visit the sick in hospitals, convalescent hospitals, and in their homes, throughout the year.

Brotherhood Ministry: Brotherhood meetings are held on the first and fourth Tuesday of each month. The Bible, and the Baptist Layman, are the main sources of study. Members of the Brotherhood visit the sick, and transport families who have no other means of transportation, to doctor appointments.

Senior Choir Ministry: Sings at convalescent hospitals, and had an outreach at the Santa Maria City Park where lunch was provided. Those in attendance at the park and in the surrounding area enjoyed the Gospel of Jesus Christ in song. The choir has also performed on the Christmas Program at Saint Louis De Montfort Catholic Church. These events showcase their choir uplifting the Lord in song.

Male Chorus Ministry: The Male Chorus ministers in song every fourth Sunday at New Hope. They participated November 1, 2007, in the National Peace Week Celebration in Santa Maria, which was held at the Foursquare Church. In this event all denominations came together to share their "Ministry of Music" and prayer for our city, our churches, and our nation.

Noonday Prayer Service: This is held every Wednesday at noon at the church. Members of New Hope, as well as other community churches, come together for an hour to pray for others and study about why we pray for others and ourselves.

Family Night and Bible Study: Held every Wednesday night. It consists of a complete meal which is served from 6-7 p.m. Children who have homework can bring it to the church and complete it. From 7-8 p.m. Bible study is held. Study groups consist of: children, youth, young adults and adults.

Children's Ministry: Meets every Wednesday night for Bible activities. Each Sunday during the morning worship they meet as a separate group away from the adults for Bible study and activities.

Youth and Young Adult Ministry: Meets every Wednesday night during Family Night & Bible Study. Their first annual "Walk it Out, Talk it Out" youth summit occurred March 15, 2008, at New Hope.

LEADERSHIP ROSTER

Pastor and First Lady: Reverend Henry L. Lewis, Jr. and Sister Agatha Lewis
Associate Minister: Anthony King
Music Minister: Ava King
Facilitator for Wednesday Noonday Bible Study: Sister Joann Green

DEACONS	DEACONESSES
Fred Washington	Beverly Washington
Willis Moore	Paula Irving
Artis (J.C.) Hawkins	Idella Moore
Jonathan Irving	Maria Castillo
Sam Castillo	
A. J. Washington	

PRAYER IS THE KEY TO HEAVEN, BUT FAITH UNLOCKS THE DOOR.

MAY YOU WALK IN FAITH

NEW HOPE MISSIONARY BAPTIST CHURCH WOMEN.
Annual Women's Day, February 15, 2009.

ANNUAL MEN'S DAY.
The men of New Hope Missionary Baptist Church gather for this photograph on June 26, 2011.

NEW HOPE MISSIONARY BAPTIST CHURCH
416 West Mill Street
Santa Maria, CA 93458
Phone: (805) 922-3119
E-mail: newhopembc1@yahoo.com